INTRODUCTION TO
BOBBIN LACE STITCHES

Bridget M Cook
&
Geraldine Stott

B T Batsford Ltd, London

By the same authors:
The Book of Bobbin Lace Stitches (Batsford, 1980)
100 Traditional Bobbin Lace Patterns (Batsford, 1982)

First published 1983
© Bridget M Cook & Geraldine Stott 1983

ISBN 0 7134 4261 1 (cased)
          4262 X (limp)

Typeset by Tek-Art Ltd, West Wickham, Kent
Printed in Great Britain by
R.J. Acford
Chichester, Sussex
for the publishers,
B T Batsford Ltd,
4 Fitzhardinge Street,
London, W1H 0AH

INTRODUCTION

This book contains a selection of the most frequently used lace stitches which have been developed in the traditional art of bobbin lace making since the seventeenth century, and is designed to aid all lace makers in the recognition and working of each individual feature. The degree of accuracy and detail is the result of many years' painstaking research into the methods used in the lace making centres of Britain and Europe, and the authors have re-discovered a wealth of stitch variations from handmade lace in museums and private collections, examining each piece to see how the particular effect was achieved.

The 86 stitches and variations are described, ranging from the simplest to the most complex; nets, grounds, fillings and decorative features are included. The content has been so arranged that all the information for each stitch — the photographs, prickings, diagrams and written instruction — can be viewed on a single page, making this book eminently practical for the working lace maker and student.

A special feature is the use of a grid background for the pricking, showing the positions of the pins around which the threads are twisted, which will allow the design to be enlarged or reduced to the reader's requirements by transference to a larger or smaller grid. The concise, step-by-step instructions and close-up illustrations showing the finished positions of the threads will enable the worker to execute each stitch with confidence and achieve a professional result.

This handy work of reference will assist all lace makers in widening their repertoire of stitches, and will provide scope for designers to create their own free patterns, as well as to use traditional prickings with a greater degree of flexibility.

(iv)

Scale Immediately below is illustrated, in actual size, a strip of eighteenth-century Flemish lace, while at the foot of the page the photograph is enlarged to the same scale as all the enlargements of all the stitches illustrated in the book. This should enable the reader to appreciate the relationship between the two when working the actual stitches.

The stitches illustrated in this piece of lace are as follows:

1 Half stitch ground
2 Twelve thread armure
3 Haloed spider
4 Toile star

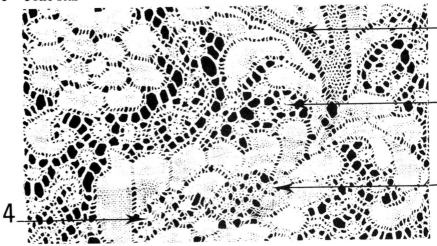

GLOSSARY

braid	A 4 thread plait made by continuous half stitches (fig. 1).	 **1.**
braid x	Number of half stitches per braid, e.g. braid x 3 means 3 half stitches, braid x 3½ means 3 half stitches plus a cross, so braid ends up untwisted.	
brick	1 pair weaving back and forth with winkie pins both sides. The worker of a brick always works over the first hole to the opposite hole, then weaves back and forth (fig. 2).	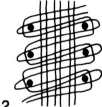 **2.**
brides	Also called legs — connecting bars, either twisted or braided. Literal translation means 'bridges'.	
bud star	Star motif with centre filled diagonally (fig 3).	
cross	Cross left hand thread over right hand thread.	**3.**
diag.	Diagonal.	
fish	With joint top and bottom having horizontal bars weaving through (fig. 4).	
h.s.	Half stitch, also called lattice stitch or gauze stitch: 2 over 3; 2 over 1; 4 over 3. Figures on diagram refer to positions only, not to the bobbins, therefore they must be recounted before each move (fig. 5).	 **4.**
honeycomb stitch	Half stitch, twist 1, pin, half stitch, twist 1 (fig. 6).	**1 2 3 4**
horiz.	Horizontal.	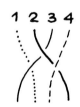
lazy join	Also called a windmill; made with 4 pairs — each pair used as a single thread, make a wholestitch (fig. 7).	**5.**

6.

7.

leaf, leaves	Also called petals or wheat ears; usually start and finish with wholestitch to create the distinctive tight top and bottom (fig. 8).
legs	As brides — connecting bars, either twisted or braided.
1t hd	Left hand.
rt hd	Right hand.
no., nos	Number, numbers.
passives	Inactive pairs through which the worker passes.
pea	Cross between fish and spider with a pair worked in and out at centre, to complete the pattern (fig. 9).
picots — single	Make a loop by twisting the thread round a pin over and towards you (fig. 10).
picots — double	Left handed picots: tw. 3 left hand pair, pin pointing to left over left hand thread, bring thread round pin, next take right hand thread round the pin in clockwise motion, gently pull all the twists round pin, tw. 2 (fig. 11).
	Right handed picots: as above but reversed and pin *under* thread (fig. 12).
picots — knotted	(fig. 13).

8.

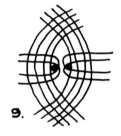

9.

10.

11.

12.

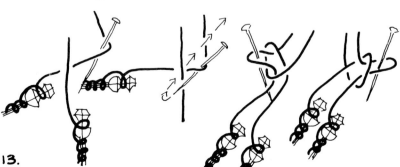

13.

pinchain	Using 2 pairs: half stitch, twist 1, pin, half stitch, twist 1 continuously along a single line (fig. 14).
pr, prs	Pair, pairs.
plait	Three threaded plait (fig. 15).

14.

raised tallies	Make an extra long leaf, pin, leave to one side, work pattern for underneath; with small stick, raise up leaf and remove pin from start and place between leaf pairs, replace pin in same hole.
ribbon	Usually a collection of untwisted passives making a decorative design.
rt hd	Right hand.
lt hd	Left hand.

15.

sewings	Joining one section to another by using a hook or needlepin to pull a loop through pin-hole of worked side then threading the other bobbin of the worker pair through the loop (fig. 16).
sewings — double	Pull 2 loops through pinhole of worked side and thread the other 2 bobbins through loops.
shell star	Star motif with pairs entering and leaving to create a hole in the central area (fig. 17).
six thread cross	Cross centre 2 threads, pass top horizontal thread over and under twice, twist both diagonal pairs, then bottom horizontal thread under and over twice, twist middle 2 threads (fig. 18). This method can also be used in same manner to cross 6 pairs.
spiders	Wholestitch all left hand pairs through right hand pairs, pin, then wholestitch all right hand pairs through left hand pairs (fig. 19).

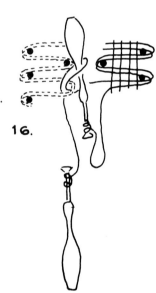

16.

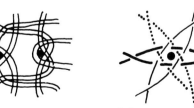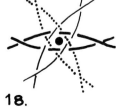

17.   **18.**   **19.**

stars	Divided into groups — toiles, shells, buds, and peas.	

stars — Divided into groups — toiles, shells, buds, and peas.

st. — Stitch.

tallies — Also called leadworks and cutworks (fig. 20).

toile star — Wholestitch star without pins (fig. 21).

tw. — Twist — right hand thread over left hand thread.

vert. — Vertical.

20.

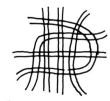

wholestitch block — 1 pair weaving back and forth with winkie pins both sides; the worker always works *under* first right hand pin and ends on left hand side (fig. 22).

winkie pin — Decorative hole made by twisting worker pair round pin (usually twice) at side of work (fig. 23).

21.

worker — The active pair — also called leaders or weavers.

w.s. — Wholestitch, also called cloth-stitch (fig. 24):
2 over 3; 2 over 1;
4 over 3; 2 over 3

Little dashes on prickings denote number of twists.

Empty circles denote temporary pins to be removed as soon as possible.

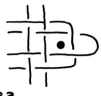

22.

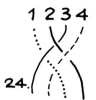

23.

1 2 3 4

24.

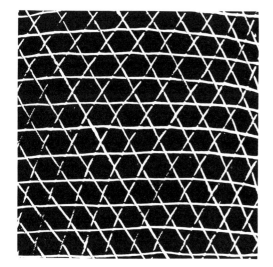

This stitch is also called Lattice stitch

2 over 3, 2 over 1, 4 over 3

these figures refer to positions, not to the threads, therefore they must be recounted after each move

If you tw. 1 at edge pins the same thread weaves back and forth

if you tw. 2 at edge pins a new thread weaves each row

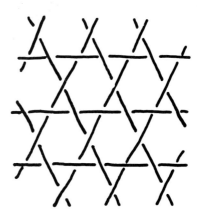

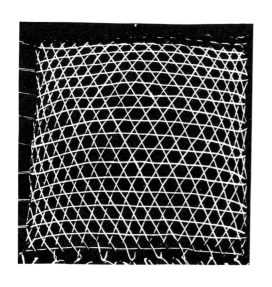

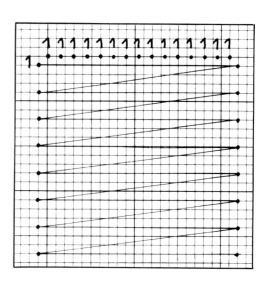

TORCHON GAUZE

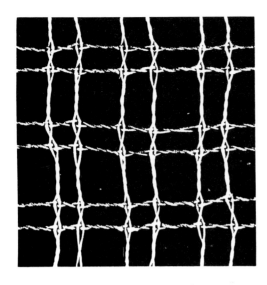

tw. 1 on short square

tw. 4 on long lines

w.s., with pin in middle at all joins

all pins removed after 2 rows, so as not
    to leave pinholes

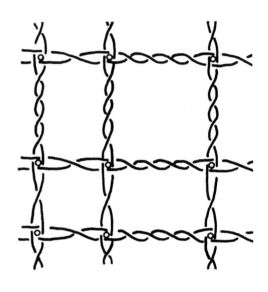

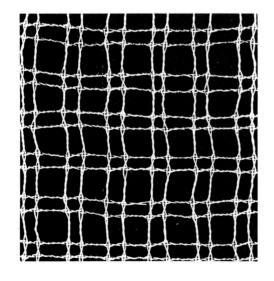

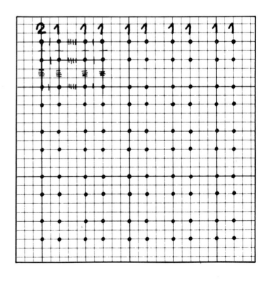

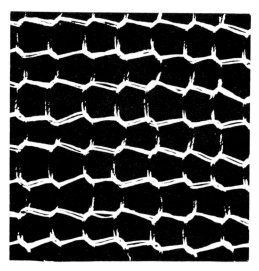

GARTER STITCH

first row (left to right) lt over rt, pin,
   lt over rt

second row (right to left) rt over lt, pin,
   rt over lt

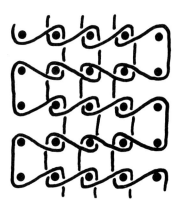

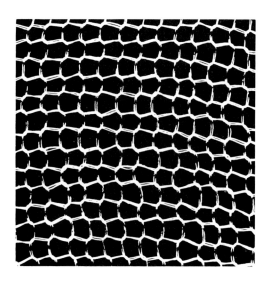

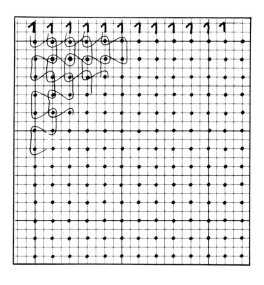

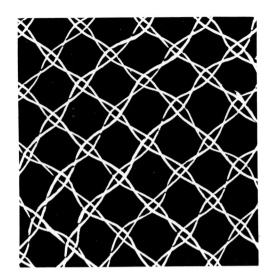

TORCHON GROUND

If made with extra twist between pins this
is called Dieppe ground.

h.s., pin, h.s.

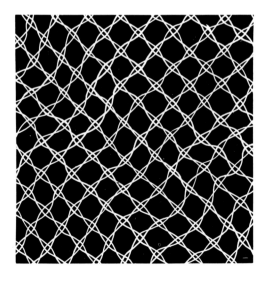

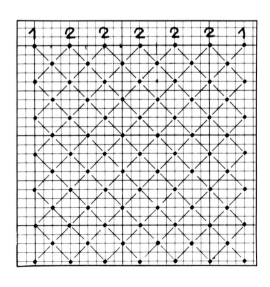

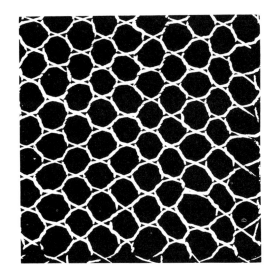

BUCKINGHAM POINT GROUND

This stitch, also called tulle or Lille ground, can be made with only one twist after each h.s. for a very fragile ground, or with three twists for a firm ground.

When this point is worked with tallies in the ground the resulting net is called Point D'Esprit.

h.s., tw. 2, pin between the pairs

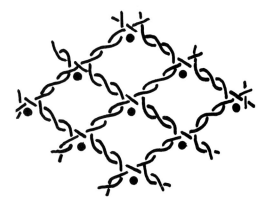

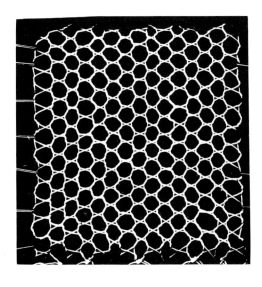

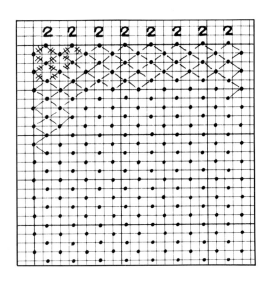

6

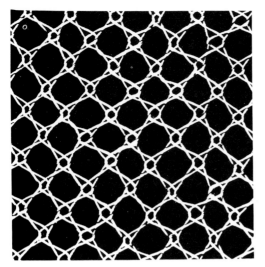

TWISTED HALF STITCH GROUND

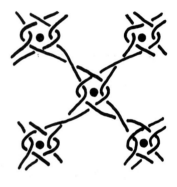

tw. 1 all legs to begin

h.s., tw. 1, pin, h.s. at each joint

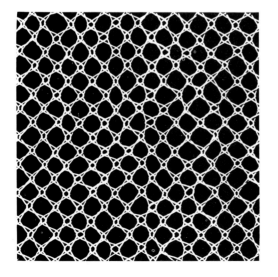

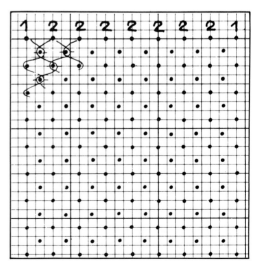

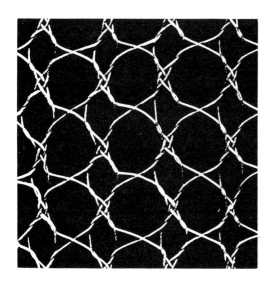

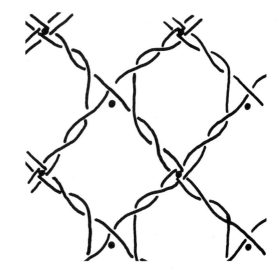

first row and every alternate row:
    h.s., pin, h.s., tw. 1

second row etc:
    h.s., pin, tw. 1

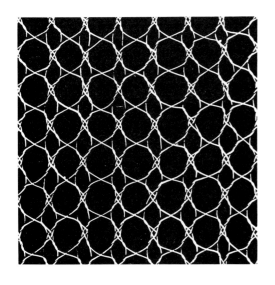

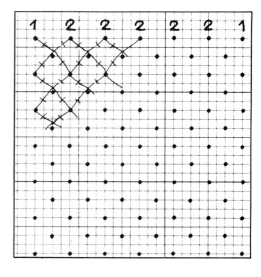

TULLE DU PUY

diagonals: tw. 1

joints: w.s., pin, w.s.

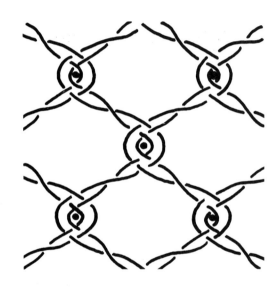

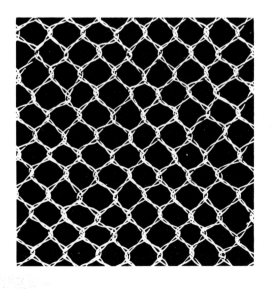

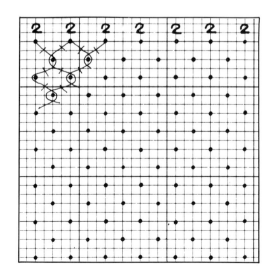

FLEMISH GROUND

at each pinhole (4 prs per pinhole) —

  w.s., tw. 1 middle 2 prs
  pin,

  h.s. 2 lt hd prs
  h.s. 2 rt hd prs

  w.s., tw. 1 middle 2 prs

  h.s. 2 lt hd prs
  h.s. 2 rt hd prs

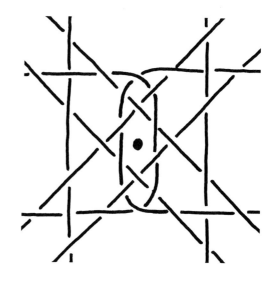

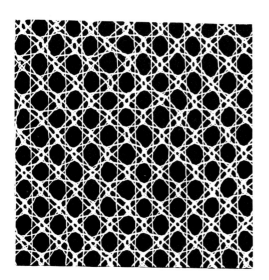

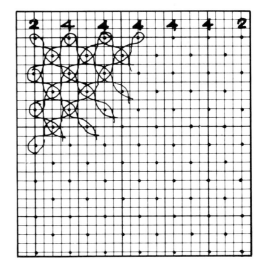

MECHLIN NET

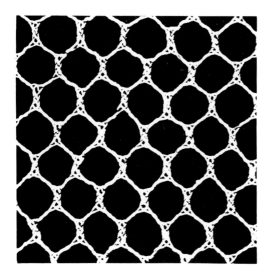

braid x 4

tw. 2 both prs at bottom of braids

divide prs and with pr from adjacent braid
make braid of next row

should be made with no pins, but when a
large area is to be filled it is best to
use temporary pins at top and bottom
of braids and remove pins as soon as
possible

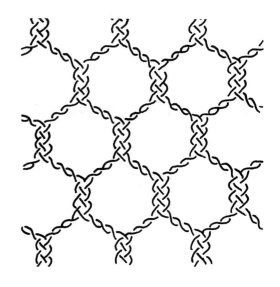

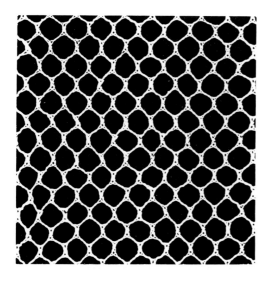

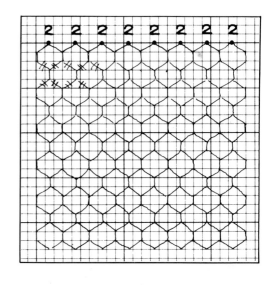

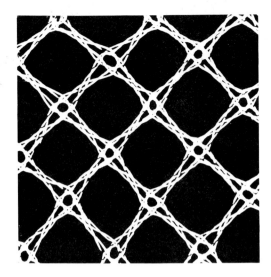

CANE GROUND

This can also be made with three twists throughout: four pins are then needed in the corners of the squares to support it.

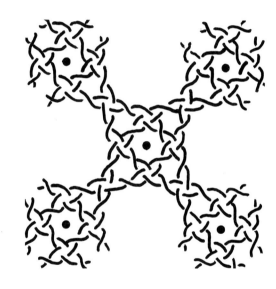

w.s., tw. 1 throughout

put pin in centre hole only

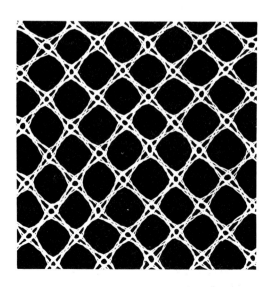

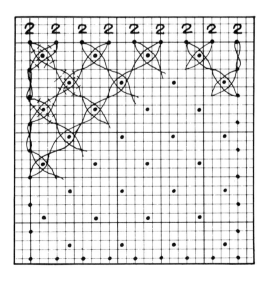

COBWEB

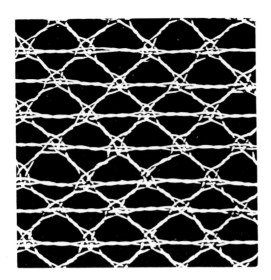

Cobweb stitch is also sometimes called Boule de Neige or Fausse Valenciennes.

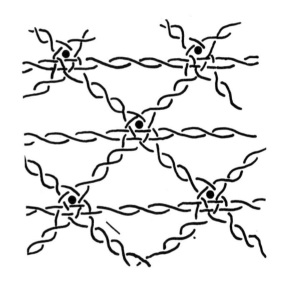

tw. 3 to start all diagonals

h.s., pin each set of 2 diag. prs

w.s. horizontal bar through these prs, tw. 3

work horizontal bar lt to rt one row, and rt to lt next row

h.s., tw. 2 diagonal prs

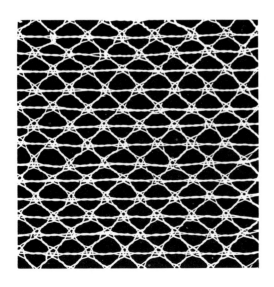

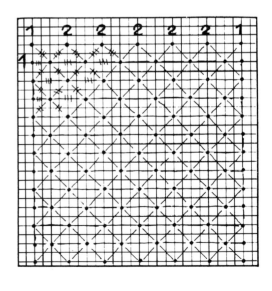

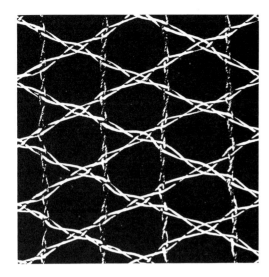

KAT STITCH

Kat stitch is also sometimes called star mesh or double ground.

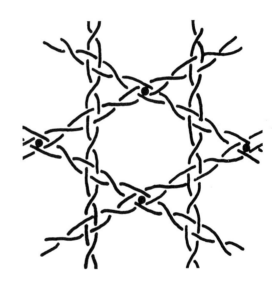

1 tw. between each joint

joint: w.s. with pin in middle

remove pins after 2 rows so as not to leave pinholes

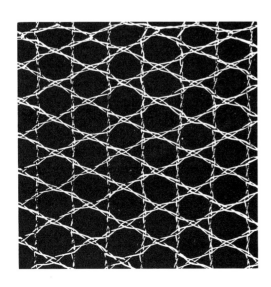

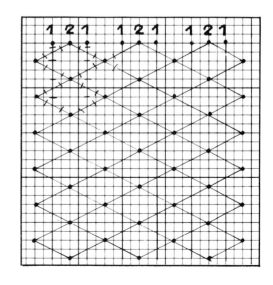

HONEYCOMB NET

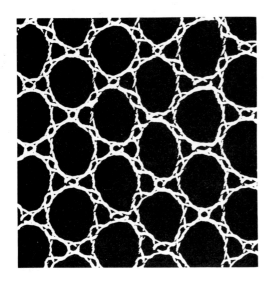

h.s., tw. 1, pin, h.s., tw. 1 (honeycomb
    stitch) at every pinhole

work continuous diag. line first

then intermediate rows, honeycomb
    stitch individual prs together

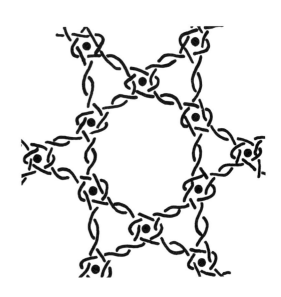

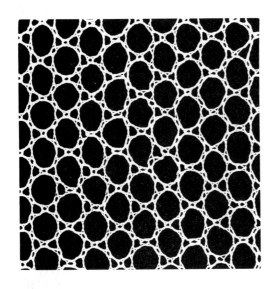

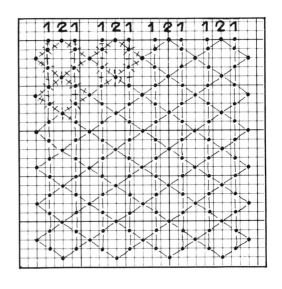

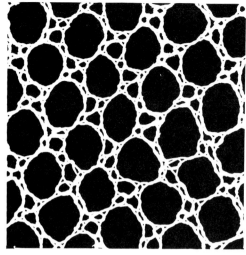

h.s., tw. 1, pin, h.s., tw. 1 (honeycomb
  stitch) at every pinhole

work continuous diagonal line first

then intermediate rows, honeycomb st.
  individual prs together

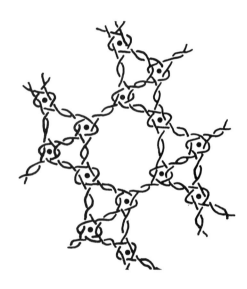

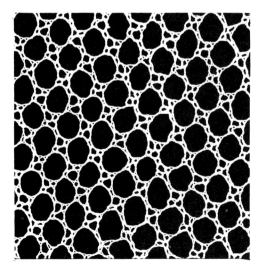

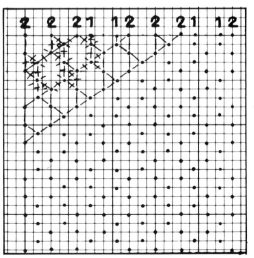

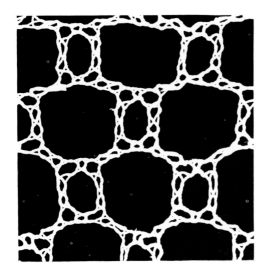

HONEYCOMB AND PINCHAIN

h.s., tw. 1, pin, h.s., tw. 1 at all pinholes
    except A, B, C and D

at A, B, C and D pin, h.s., tw. 1

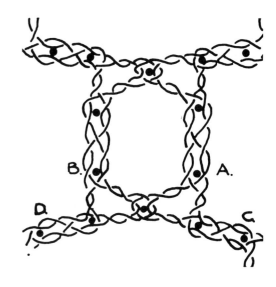

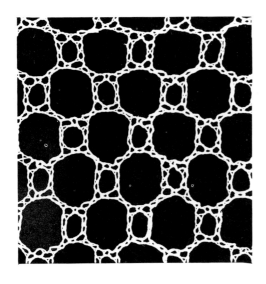

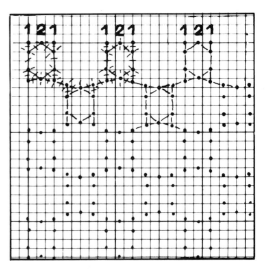

BRAID AND LOCK STITCH

braid each leg

tw. 3 inside prs

with corresponding pr from adjacent
  braid: w.s., tw. 1, pin, w.s., tw. 3

tw. 1 outside pr

braid to next lock stitch

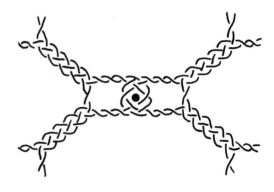

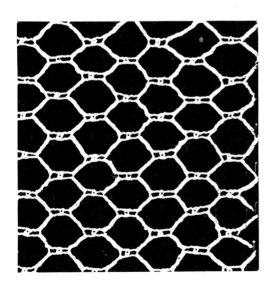

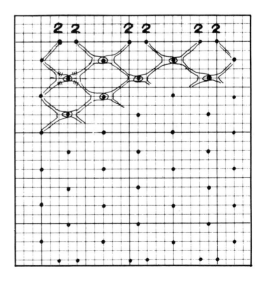

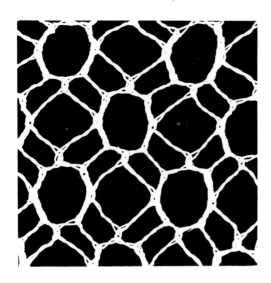

RINGS

tw. 3 all leg prs between rings

at top of ring — w.s., pin, w.s., tw. 1

lt hd side — w.s., pin, h.s. x 3½

with outside pr of braid and leg — w.s., pin, w.s.

tw. 3 leg pr, leave

tw. 2 inside pr

with inside prs — h.s. x 3½, pin, w.s., tw. 3 leg, tw. 1 inner pr.

repeat on rt hd side

base of ring — w.s., pin, w.s., tw. 3 both prs

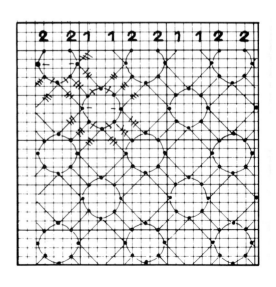

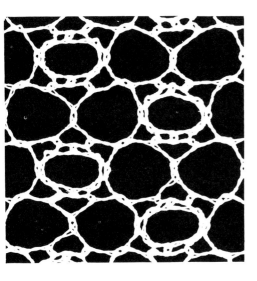

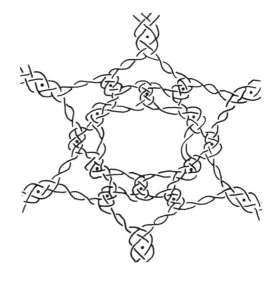

tw. 2 the pairs leading to and from the outer points of the star before and after they cross

w.s., tw. 1, pin, w.s.

at all other pinholes around the inner circle — w.s., tw. 1, pin, w.s., tw. 1

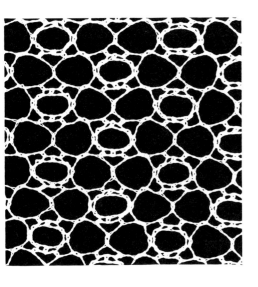

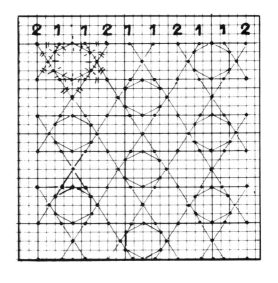

20

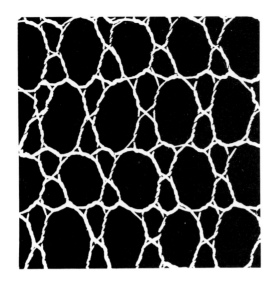

DEVONSHIRE HONEYCOMB VARIATION

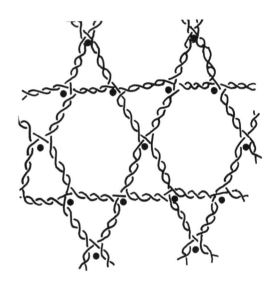

h.s., tw. 3 at each pinhole

horizontal line weaves back and forth
every alternate row

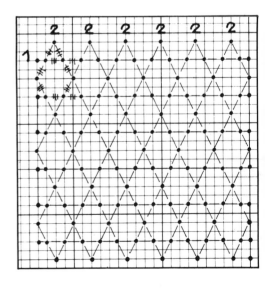

SIX SIDED BOBBIN MESH

braid x 10½

sew top pr over middle of loop above,
  pin, gently pull threads to correct
  distance between loops, then sew round
  this newly formed loop

note: very difficult to keep tidy

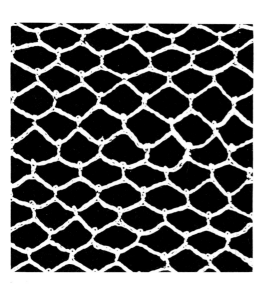

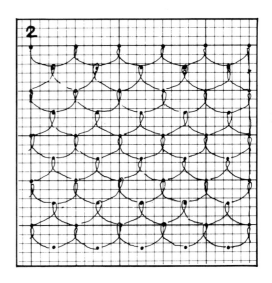

FEATHER GROUND

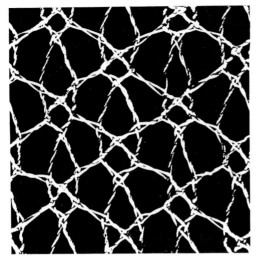

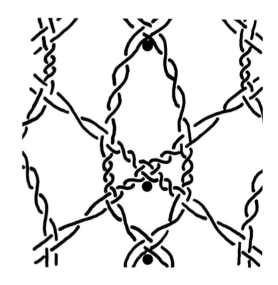

all joints are w.s.

supporting pins are placed under crossings

tw. 2 within feather

tw. 1 diagonals outside feather

feather: tw. 3 top two sections and tw. 1 bottom section

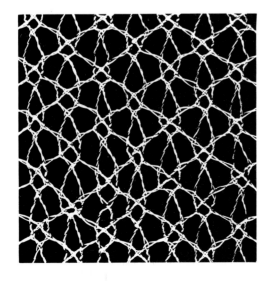

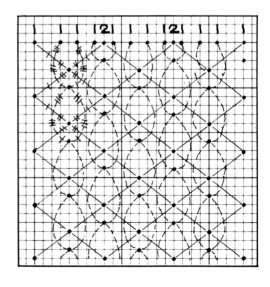

TRIANGULAR GROUND

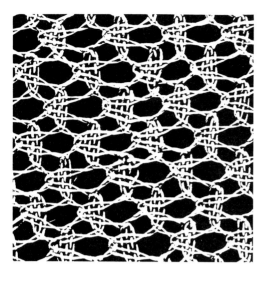

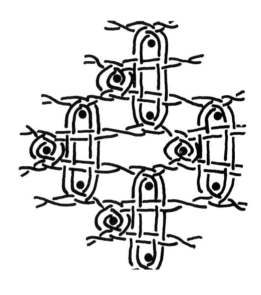

w.s. throughout

pin to support top and bottom of lozenge

w.s., pin, w.s. at apex of triangle

tw. 1 between triangles

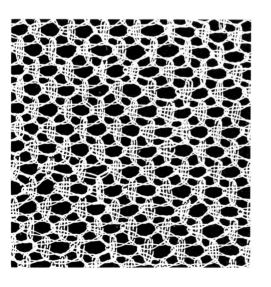

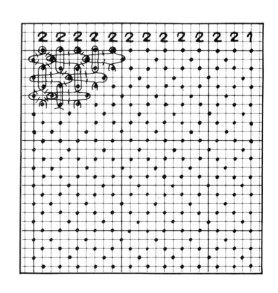

BIAS GROUND A

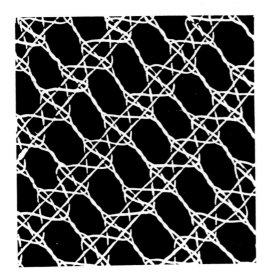

3, 4, 5, 6 = 4 pin block

```
    1 3 2
4   ◇   5
    7 6 8
```

1, 2, 7, 8 = intervening stitches

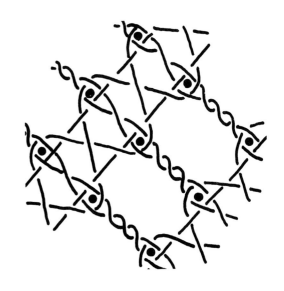

work on diagonal only

4 pin block: h.s., pin, h.s. at 3, 5, 4 and
   6, but work h.s. 2 middle prs between
   the pins numbered 4 and 5

h.s. 2 lt hd prs between blocks

tw. 3 each pr between rows

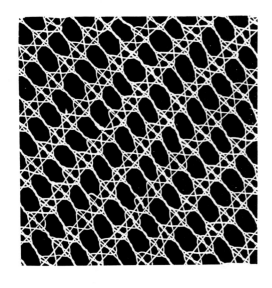

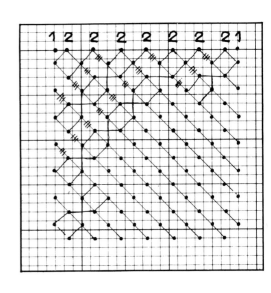

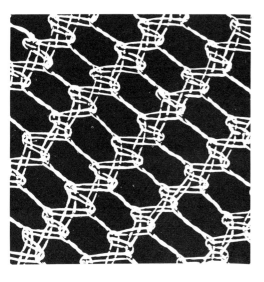

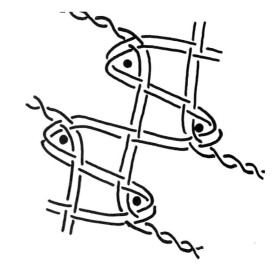

work on the diagonal only

w.s., tw. 1 worker pr, pin, w.s.

w.s. through passives

tw. 3 between rows

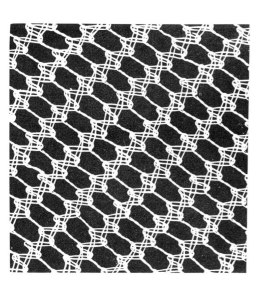

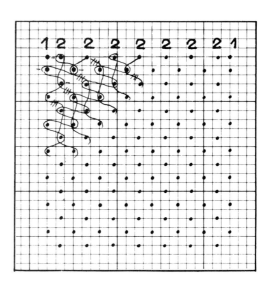

BIAS GROUND C

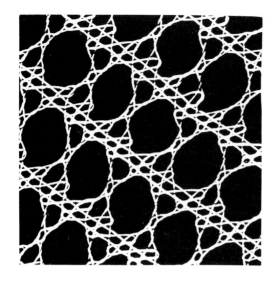

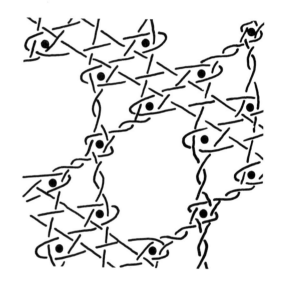

h.s. back and forth down diagonals, picking
  up prs on rt hd side and leaving out
  prs on lt hd side; tw. 1 round pins at
  sides

tw. 1 all prs before crosses

h.s., tw. 1, pin, h.s., tw. 1 at pinholes
  between diagonals

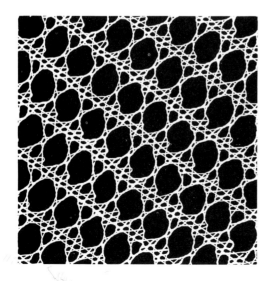

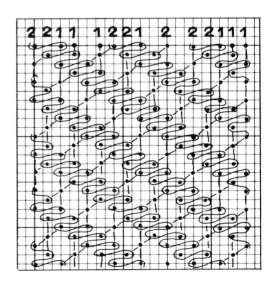

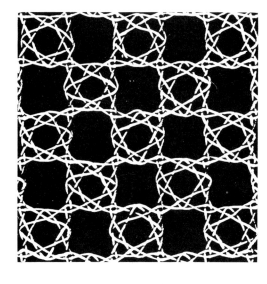

ROSE GROUND A

3, 4, 5, 6 = 4 pin block

```
        1 3 2
   4      ◇      5
        7 6 8
```

1, 2, 7, 8 = intervening stitches

Although Rose Ground can be worked as described below, it can also be created entirely in half stitches, whole stitches or a mixture of the two to give different forms of Rose Ground.

4 pin block: h.s., pin, h.s.

intervening stitches: w.s., tw. 1 (no pin)

spaces and blocks alternated each row

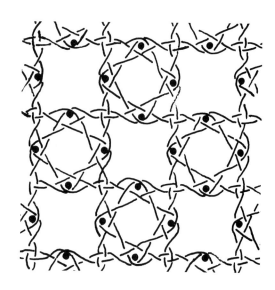

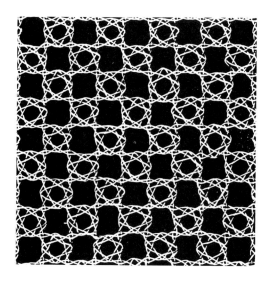

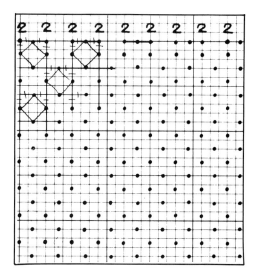

ROSE GROUND B

3, 4, 5, 6 = 4 pin block

$$4 \quad \begin{array}{c} 1\ 3\ 2 \\ \diamondsuit \\ 7\ 6\ 8 \end{array} \quad 5$$

1, 2, 7, 8 = intervening stitches

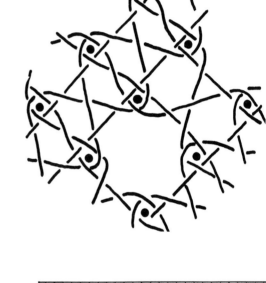

worked on diagonal only

4 pin block: h.s., pin, h.s.

work in this sequence
    pinhole 3
    pinhole 5
    work h.s. 2 middle prs between 4 & 5
    pinhole 4
    pinhole 6

intervening stitches:
    h.s.

blocks and spaces alternate each row

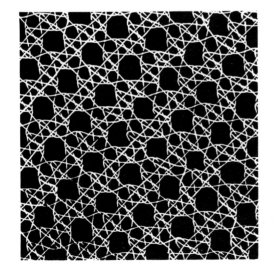

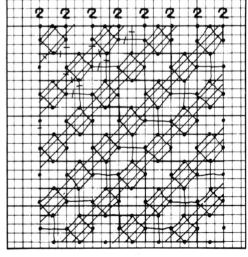

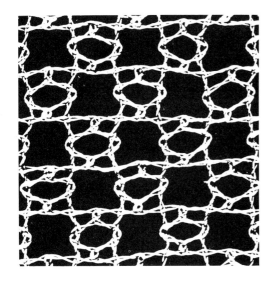

ROSE GROUND C

3, 4, 5, 6 = 4 pin block

```
    1 3 2
4   ◇   5
    7 6 8
```

1, 2, 7, 8 = intervening stitches

4 pin block: w.s., tw. 1, pin, w.s., tw. 1

intervening stitches: w.s., with tw. 1
  after it

spaces and blocks alternated each row

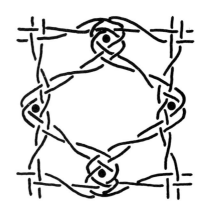

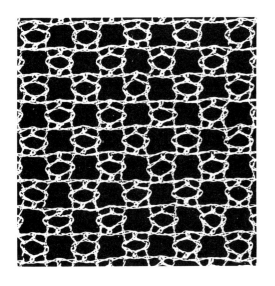

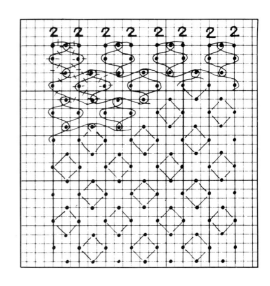

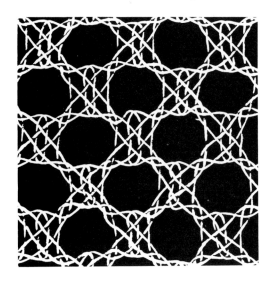

ROSE GROUND D

3, 4, 5, 6 = 4 pin block

```
      1 3 2
   4  ◇  5
      7 6 8
```

1, 2, 7, 8 = intervening stitches

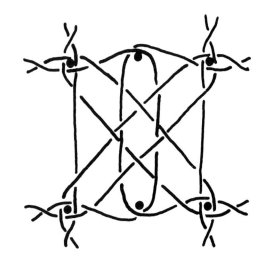

4 pin block:
    3 and 6 — h.s., pin, h.s.
    4 and 5 — h.s.

intervening stitches: h.s., pin, h.s.

spaces and blocks alternated each row

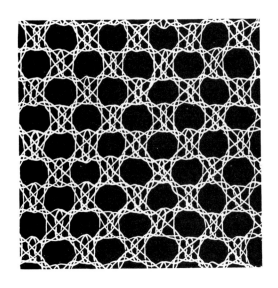

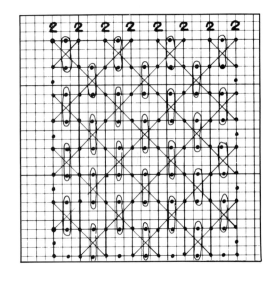

ROSE GROUND E

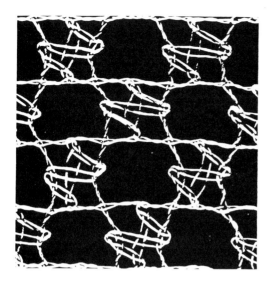

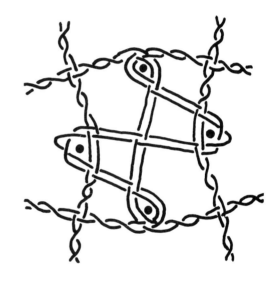

w.s. throughout

no twists in zigzag centres

tw. 2 all other horizontal and vertical
lines

tw. 2 at winkie pins

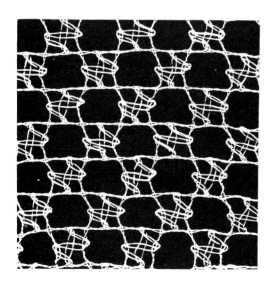

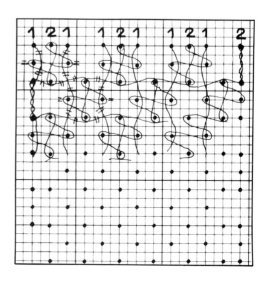

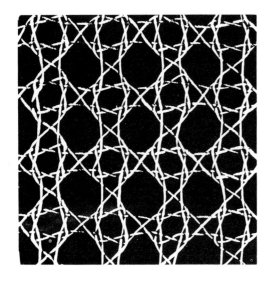

ROSE GROUND
WORKED STRAIGHT

3, 4, 5, 6 = 4 pin block

```
      1 3 2
   4  ◇  5
      7 6 8
```

1, 2, 7, 8 = intervening stitches

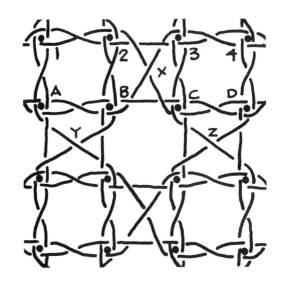

use two horizontal workers at same time

h.s., pin, h.s., 1 & 2 & A & B

with both working prs work h.s. at X

h.s., pin, h.s., 3 & 4 & C & D continue to
   end

h.s. alternate squares Y & Z

work workers back as before: alternate
   squares and crosses

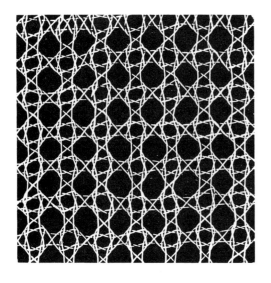

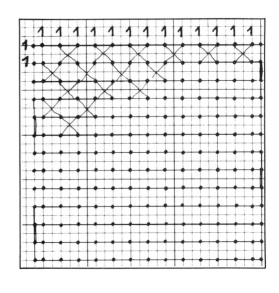

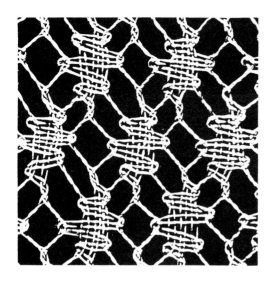

SIX LEGGED ZECCATELLO

This can also be done in half stitch.

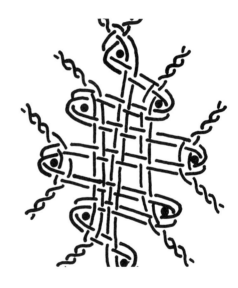

top rt hd leg — worker

w.s. back and forth picking up legs to rt and lt until all 6 legs are in use, then leave out legs lt and rt until original 2 prs

tw. 1 workers at winkie pins

tw. 3 between diamonds

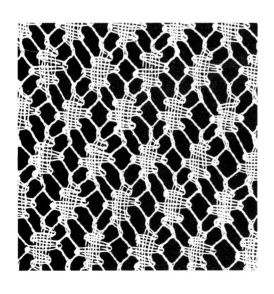

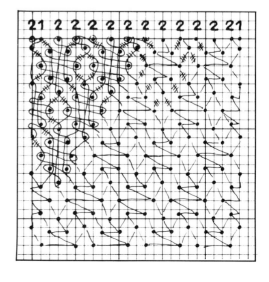

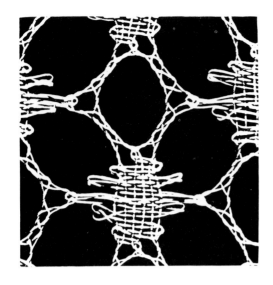

FOUR PIN MAYFLOWER WITH PINCHAIN

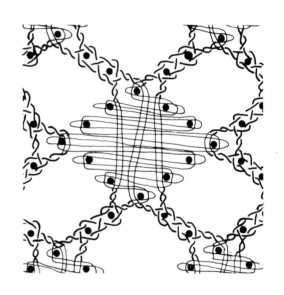

w.s. diamonds, tw. 2 workers at pinholes

tw. 2 passives and workers at bottom of diamonds

h.s., tw. 1, pin, h.s., tw. 1 at all other pinholes

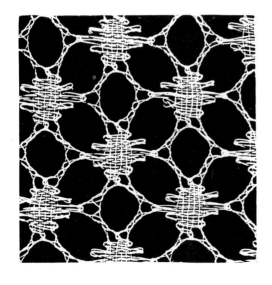

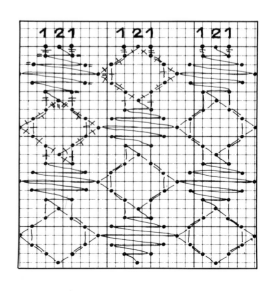

MAYFLOWER

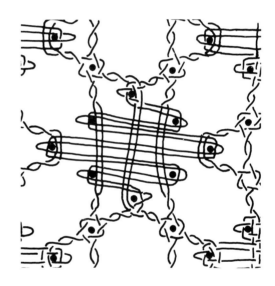

w.s. diamonds, tw. 2 workers at pinholes

tw. 2 passives and workers at bottom of diamonds

h.s., tw. 1, pin, h.s., tw. 1 at all other pinholes

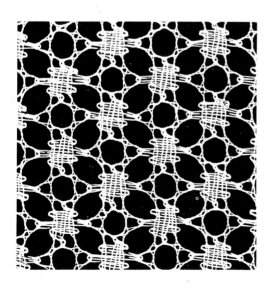

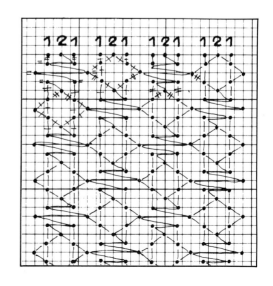

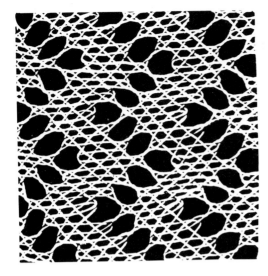

this pattern is worked horizontally in sets

rt to lt zigzag set:
    (1) repeat the following x 3 —
        5 h.s. to lt, pin,
        4 h.s. to rt, pin,

    (2) tw. 1 3 legs on rt hd side
    (3) start next rt to lt zigzag
    (4) continue until end of horiz. set

lt to rt zigzag set:
    (1) repeat the following x 3 —
        3 h.s. to lt, pin,
        4 h.s. to rt, pin

    (2) tw. 1 3 legs on lt hd side
    (3) start next lt to rt zigzag
    (4) continue until end of horiz. set

repeat these 2 sets until end

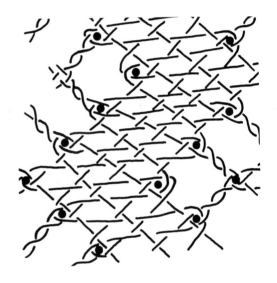

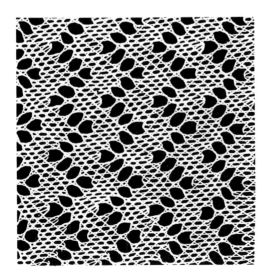

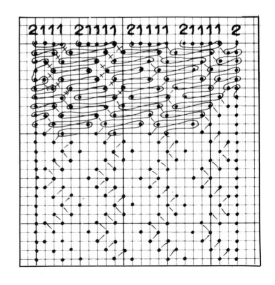

HALF STITCH DIAMONDS

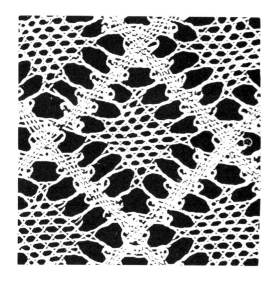

w.s. diagonal bars until 2 meet

w.s., pin, w.s.

w.s. these prs through their respective passives, tw. 1 both workers, pin and leave

w.s. all 4 passives through each other

w.s. workers back through respective passives again

w.s., pin, w.s. at bottom hole

continue w.s. back and forth, tw. 2 at each turn, adding legs one side and leaving out other side

tw. 2 all legs left out

h.s. diamond in middle

tw. 1 all legs after diamond

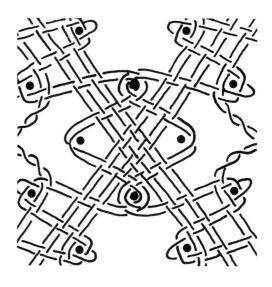

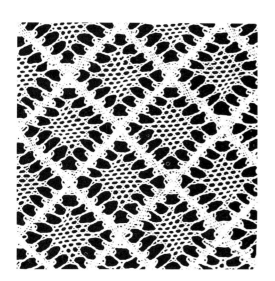

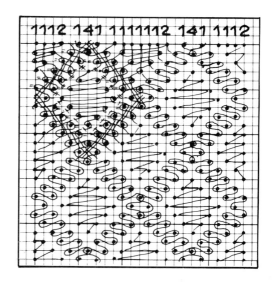

FESTOON

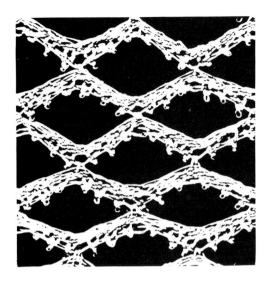

with 1 pr as workers, w.s. through 3
passives, tw. 3, w.s. 1 passive, work
picot

return through 1 passive, tw. 3, w.s. 2
passives

work turning stitch: w.s. and h.s. with
worker and last passive, then return

repeat 6 times

make sewing into centre of moon of
previous row

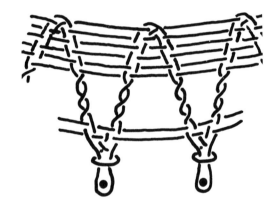

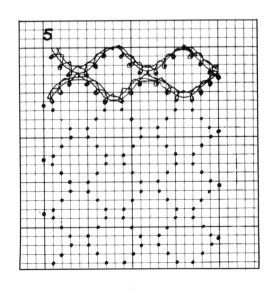

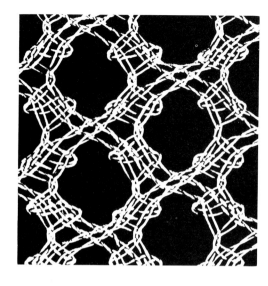

w.s., pin, w.s. each side of circle

w.s., tw. 2, w.s. at winkie pins

tw. 1, w.s., tw. 1 at grill squares top and
    bottom of circles

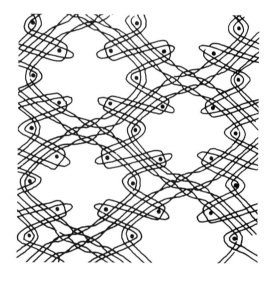

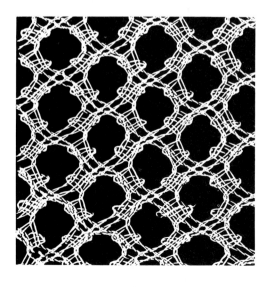

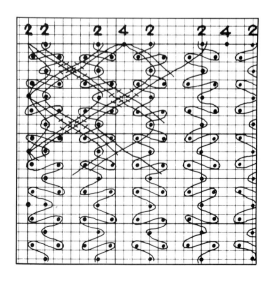

SPIDER RING

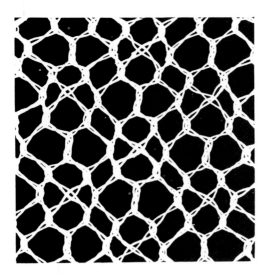

w.s., pin, w.s. at all pinholes

tw. 1 all prs around and across ring

tw. 3 all prs leading to and from one ring
and another

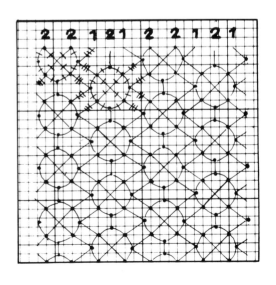

EIGHT THREAD
ARMURE – BINCHE

made in 4 pin groups throughout

h.s., pin centre 2 prs

h.s., pin 2 lt hd prs and 2 rt hd prs

h.s. centre 2 prs

h.s. 2 lt hd prs and 2 rt hd prs

h.s., pin centre 2 prs

diagram shows 4 groups

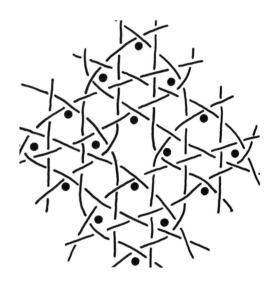

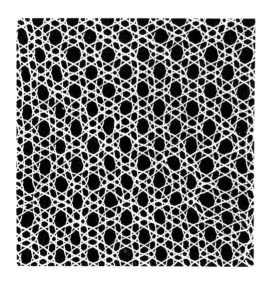

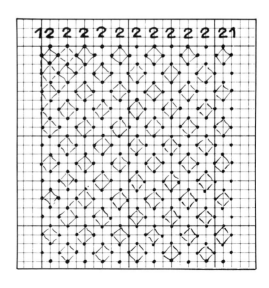

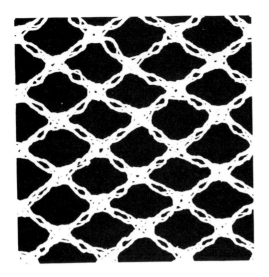

BUCKINGHAM POINT CORD GROUND

w.s., tw. 2, pin, w.s. at all pinholes

then w.s. all 4 adjacent prs through each
   other

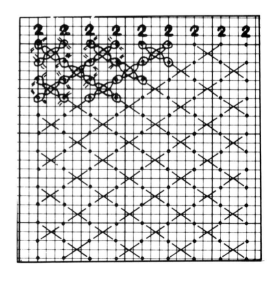

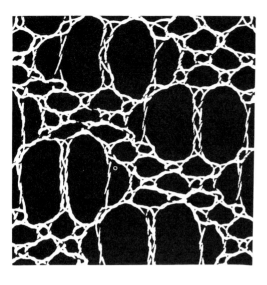

HONEYCOMB BARS AND PINCHAIN

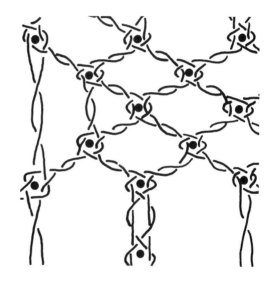

honeycomb stitch throughout:
  h.s., tw. 1, pin, h.s., tw. 1

work diagonal bars first, then pinchain
  (3 consecutive honeycomb stitches)
  and crosses as shown

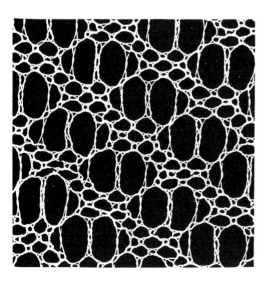

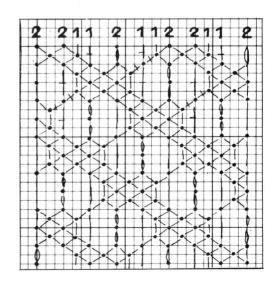

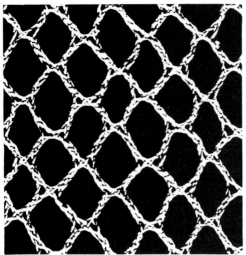

VALENCIENNES

The typical diamond look can be achieved by using this technique but with a wider pricking.

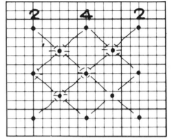

Various forms of Valenciennes net can be worked by using whole stitch, half stitch, twists or no twists at the cross-over junction.

braid 4 times

h.s., pin, h.s. centre prs

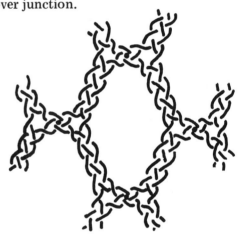

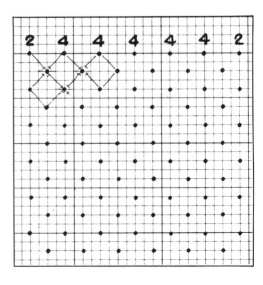

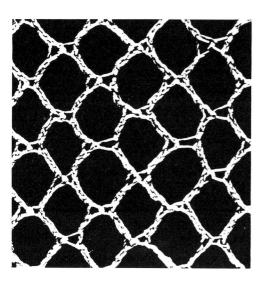

braid x 4, tw. 2 each pr

rt hd pr place pin between threads, braid x 3½, tw. 2 each pr

lt hd pr place pin between threads, braid x 3½

joint is made where next braid zigzags to meet it

tw. 1 lt hd pr — make sewing into former hole with this pr, tw. 1, idle pr tw. 2

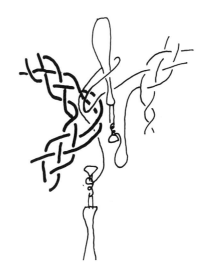

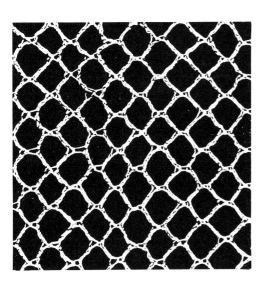

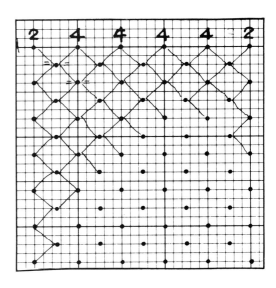

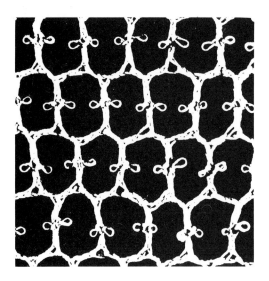

HEXAGONAL BRAID WITH PICOTS A

can only be worked diagonally, right to left

prs have to be added at rt hd side as well as at top, then tied out on lt hd side and bottom

* work down long vertical side — braid x 3½, make knotted picot each side, braid x 3½, pin between prs

braid x 3½ along the rt to lt short side

make sewing with top pr of braid into lt hd pinhole of previous row, gently pull to make sewing same length as braid x 3½

sew round this new bar again

continue until end of row

then start again at top of new row

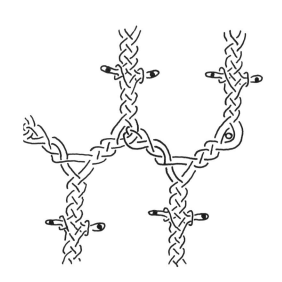

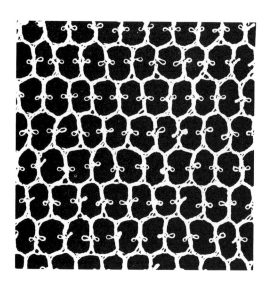

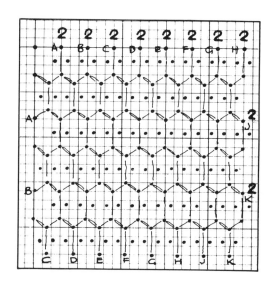

braid x 3½ between knotted picots
  throughout

start at A, braid to pinhole B, pin braid
  around it up to C, make sewing, braid
  up beyond C (this keeps sewing tight),
  then fold this braid down so that it
  rests on top of braid B-C, after picot
  on rt make sewing under lower braid
  to secure both braids together, continue
  braid to B, make another sewing at B
  and braid around pin at D — continue

not an easy pattern to keep tidy with its
  3 sewings for each vertical bride

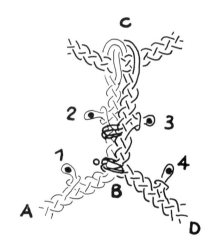

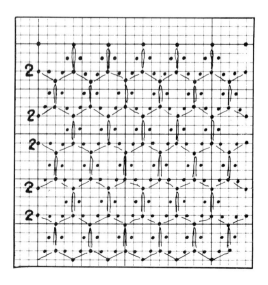

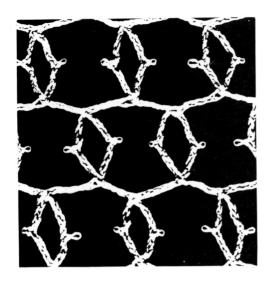

BRAIDED LEAVES

This pattern can also be made on this pricking to give a diamond effect.

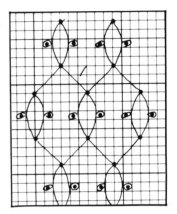

braid with knotted picots

lazy join at all junctions, with pin in
middle

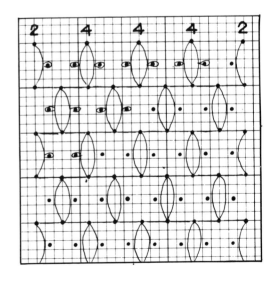

BRAIDED LEAVES WITH PICOTS

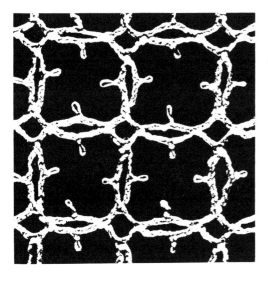

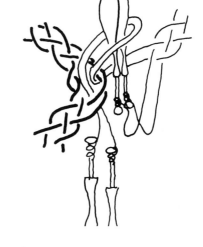

work with only one braid throughout

braid with knotted picots

tw. 2 at pinholes and continue to plait
   (this makes hole for sewing)

double sewings throughout

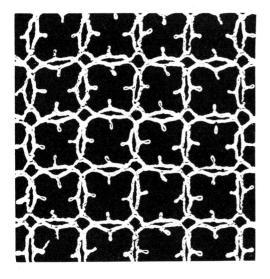

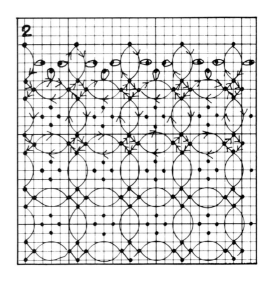

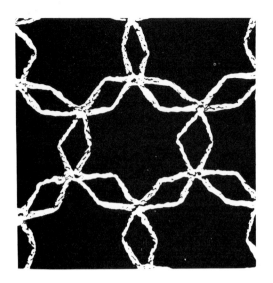

HEXAGONAL BRAIDED LEAVES

work horizontal leaves by using 2 sets
of braids, one for the rt hd and one for
the lt hd edge of leaf

make lazy join with pin in middle, at base
of leaf, continue to end of line, take
both braids down to next horizontal
line, and work back to base of vert.
leaf, using only one braid, braid up
one side of leaf and do double sewing
into the join of pr of leaves above it

braid down second side of leaf, make
another lazy join, with pin, at base as
close as possible to first lazy join of
horizontal leaf

continue

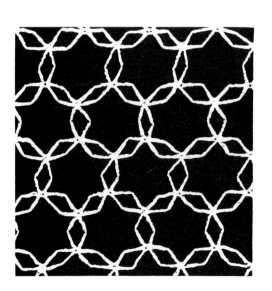

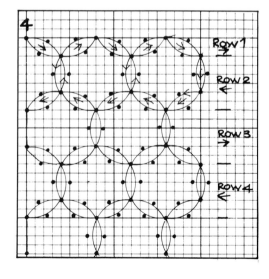

DEVONSHIRE FOUR PEARL FILLING

This filling is also sometimes called Blossom or Rose.

rt hd pr of lt hd braid, picot on right, w.s.

2 middle prs: w.s., tw. 1

2 rt hd prs: w.s., picot to the right, w.s.

2 lt hd prs: w.s., picot to the left, w.s.

2 middle prs: tw. 1, w.s.

2 rt hd prs: w.s., picot to the left

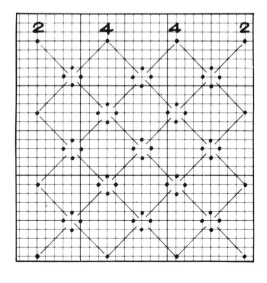

DOUBLE APPLE BLOSSOM

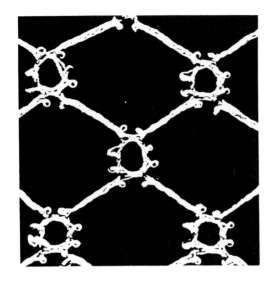

braid to pin A

work lt hd picot at A, tw. 1, w.s., repeat
    on rt hd side at B, but reversed

w.s. centre prs, tw. 1
2 lt hd prs w.s., double picot on lt, tw. 1
    w.s.
double picot again on lt, w.s., tw.1 rt hd
    pr only
repeat on rt hd side but reversed
w.s. centre prs
w.s. 2 lt hd prs double picot on rt of
    this join, tw. 1

braid

repeat on rt hd side but reversed

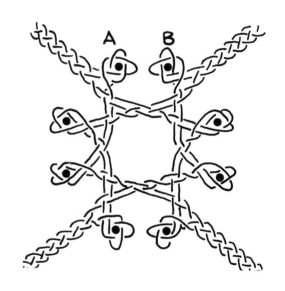

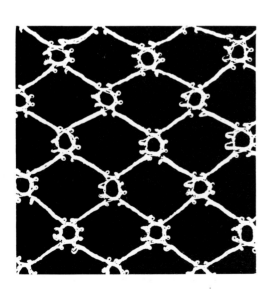

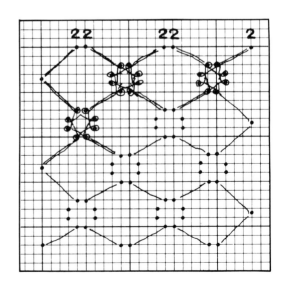

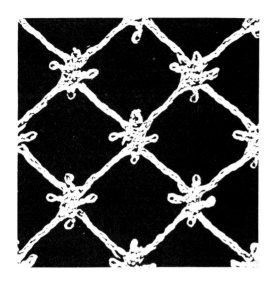

WHOLESTITCH APPLE BLOSSOM

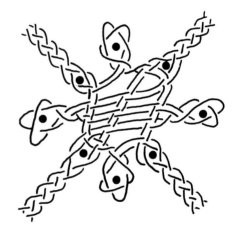

braid legs

pin between prs

lt hd pr of lt hd braid w.s., picot at top
   pin, w.s. to right, leave

w.s. 2nd from rt to lt and picot on lt
   hd side

w.s. back to right and picot on right

w.s. to left, leave

pin and take lt hd vertical w.s. to right,
   picot at bottom

w.s. to far right, pin between prs

tw. 1 all 4 prs before braiding

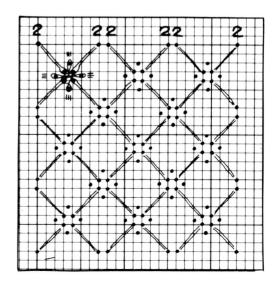

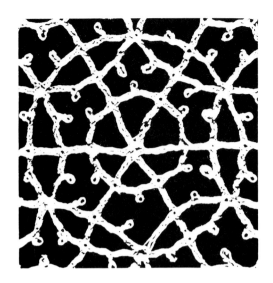

WHEEL WITH LEAVES

(2) six thread cross:
use each pr as single threads — cross
centre 2 threads, pass top horizontal
thread over and under twice, twist both
diagonal prs, pin between prs, then
bottom horizontal thread under and
over twice, twist middle 2 threads

(1) braid and double picot throughout
double sewings at lt & rt of wheel and at
top of vertical leaf
six thread cross at centre of wheel (see
above)
lazy join with pin in middle at all other
junctions; tw. 2 lower pr when there
is to be a sewing later
horizontal braid works through leaves,
then top half of wheel, through
diagonals, work back through centre
to beginning of circle, sew and complete
bottom half of circle, sew and braid to
next wheel
with 2 sets of braids work both top and
bottom line of horizontal leaves, lazy
join after each leaf, after 2nd horizontal
leaf, top pr works up lt hd side of vertical
leaf, sew into join of leaves above,
return down rt hd side, lazy join as
close to last lazy join as possible

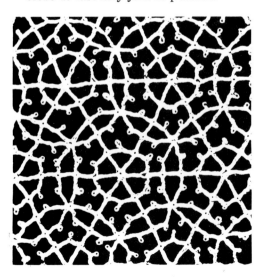

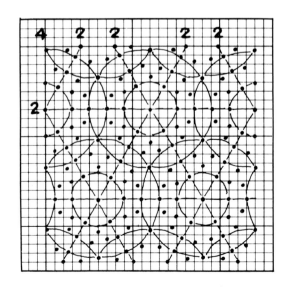

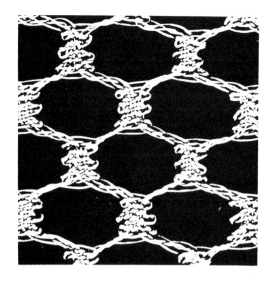

when worker has been worked from rt to lt the last time at end of brick, the worker pr is passed under passive pr and w.s. again

then that pr works across to next brick

w.s. between bricks elsewhere

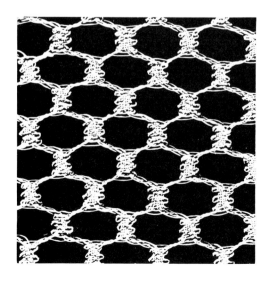

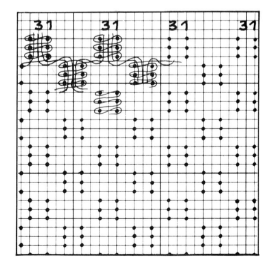

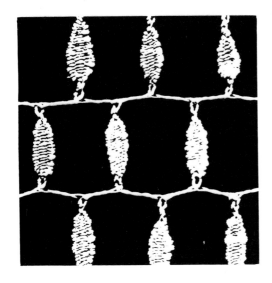

DEVONSHIRE PIN FILLING 1

This filling can also be made with square ended tallies, using the same method as below excluding the wholestitch at the top and bottom of the leaf.

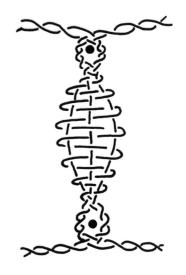

top of leaf:
   w.s., pin, tw. 3, w.s., tw. 1

weave leaf as usual

bottom of leaf:
   w.s., pin, tw. 3, w.s., tw. 3

1 pr from each leaf above makes next
   leaf below

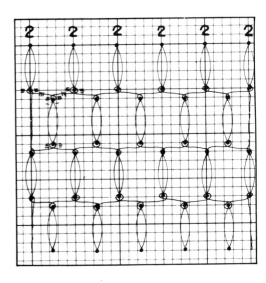

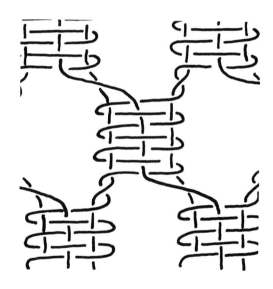

using the thread on far rt as weaver, weave back and forth ending on lt hd side

this way the weaver becomes the weaver for the next tally below left, which helps to keep its shape

tw. 2 weaver with its adjacent thread

tw. 1 bottom rt hd pr

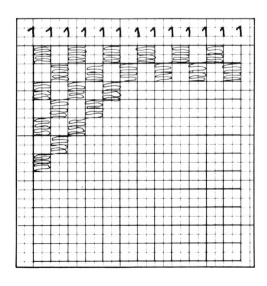

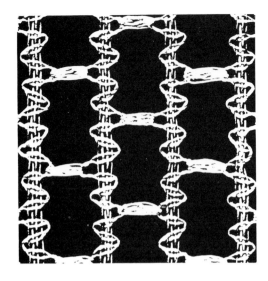

WHOLESTITCH CUCUMBER

w.s. back and forth through vertical passives

tw. 2 at winkie pins

tw. 2 before and after tallies except bottom pr with weaving thread — tw. 3

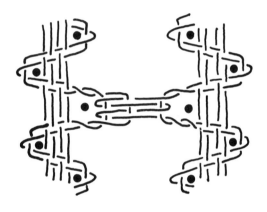

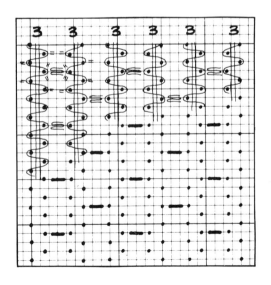

DEVONSHIRE DIAMOND FILLING

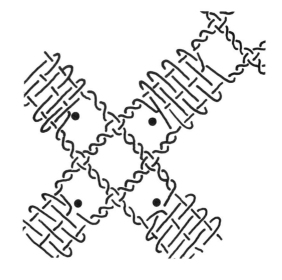

work rectangular tallies, pin at bottom of each

tw. 3 all prs

w.s., tw. 3 2 centre prs

w.s., tw. 3 2 lt hd prs, pin between prs

w.s., tw. 3 2 rt hd prs, pin between prs

w.s., tw. 3 2 centre prs

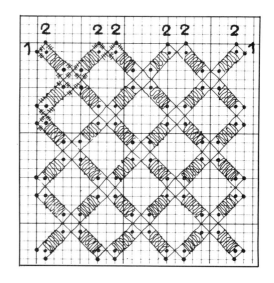

MARGUERITE À CENTRE DE TOILE

weave long thin leaves
w.s. centre through each other

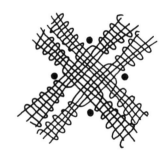

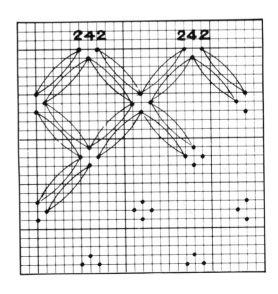

FAT MALTESE PETALS

By constructing the leaves in a fine form
the resulting work can be adapted to
create thin Cluny petals.

weave flat leaves as shown

lazy join between each 4 leaf joint

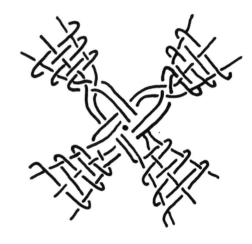

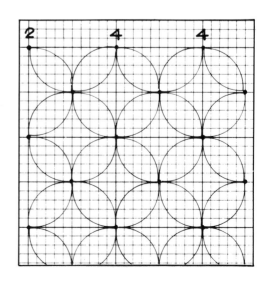

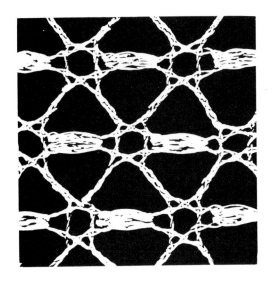

STAR CROSSING WITH TALLIES

tw. 2, w.s., tw. 2 between crossings

w.s., tw. 1 both diagonals at top of crossings

w.s., tw. 1 centre 2 prs, then w.s., tw. 1 back through vertical prs

make wide shallow tally with pr from adjacent crossing, tw. 1 both prs

w.s., tw. 1 pr from tally through vertical pr both sides

w.s., tw. 1 centre 2 prs

w.s. 2 outside prs that become next diagonals

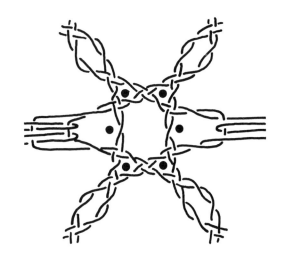

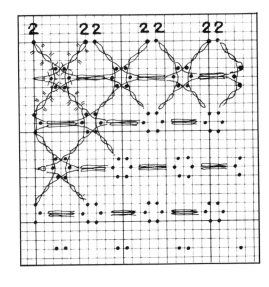

w.s., tw. 2 lattice work between tulips

weave top threads as usual until pin on
   rt, weave worker through 2 threads
   from lattice band, pin

weave to left under 1st thread, over next
   2 threads, under next thread, over next
   2 threads, and under last thread, (having
   brought in corresponding pr from
   lattice work above)

work back and forth thus using single
   and double threads until the bottom
   of tulip

w.s. 4 central threads
w.s. 2 lt hd prs
w.s. 2 rt hd prs

place temporary pins to hold shape

braid until next tulip

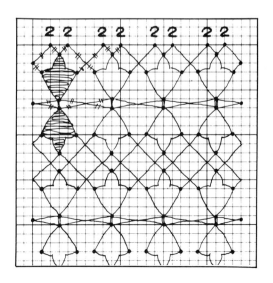

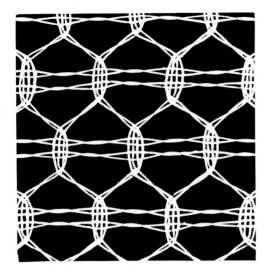

FISH WITH TWO HORIZONTALS

These fishes can be constructed with more horizontals with or without the torchon ground between them.

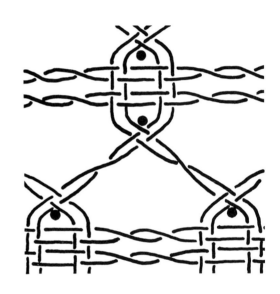

tw. 1 diag. lines

w.s., pin

w.s. horizontal bars through fish

tw. 2 between fish

pin, w.s. at bottom of fish

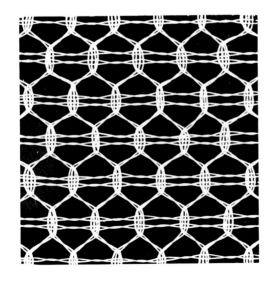

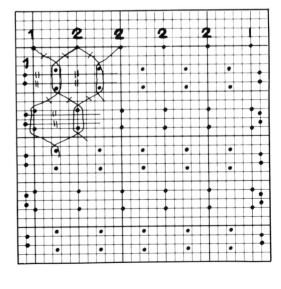

ITALIAN SPIDER WITH EYE

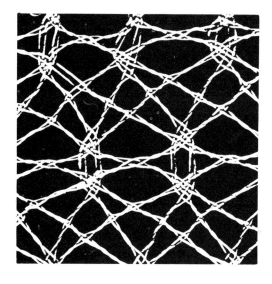

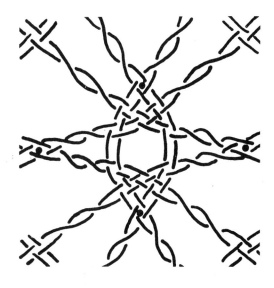

tw. 2 all diagonals

w.s. where two meet

w.s. with pin in middle at all pinholes

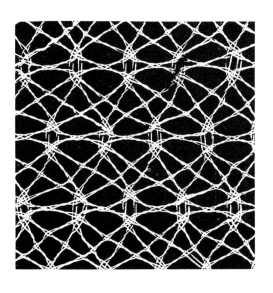

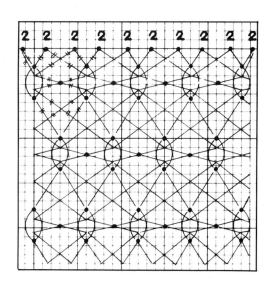

PLAIN TORCHON SPIDERS

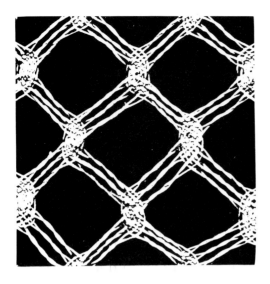

tw. 3 all legs

w.s. all lt hd prs through rt hd prs

pin

w.s. all rt hd prs through lt hd prs

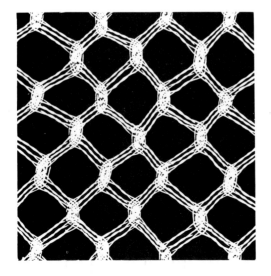

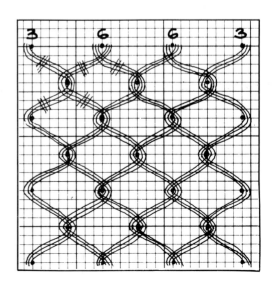

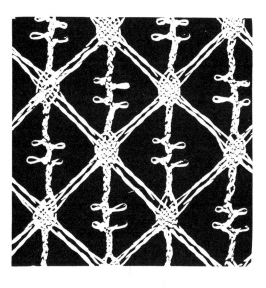

EYELESS SPIDER
WITH PICOTS

tw. 3 diagonal legs

braid verticals until picots

work knotted picots with h.s. between

braid x 4

work knotted picots with h.s. between

braid until start of spider, pin between
  prs

work eyeless spider

pin before start of next braid

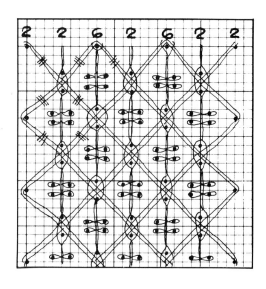

TWISTED SPIDER AND BRAID

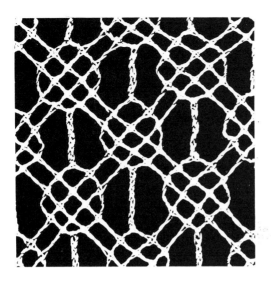

braid to top of spider

tw. 2 legs between spiders

w.s., tw. 2 throughout except far rt and
    lt of outer circle — tw. 3

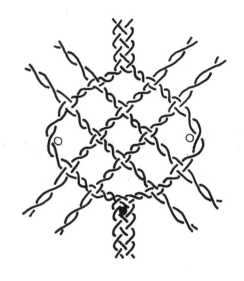

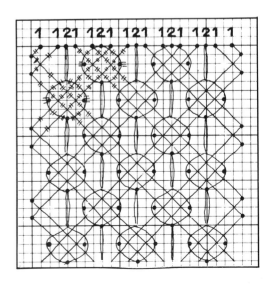

SPIDER'S EYE

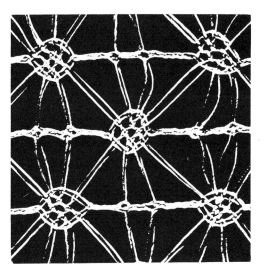

work horizontally only

braid to circle, pin and divide

w.s. top pr through diagonals and
verticals

tw. 1 all 4 prs

w.s., tw. 1 2 centre prs
w.s., tw. 1 2 lt hd prs
w.s., tw. 1 2 rt hd prs
w.s., tw. 1 2 centre prs

w.s. bottom circumference pr through
these 4 prs

pin before starting braiding

w.s. verticals through braid pin in middle
to support

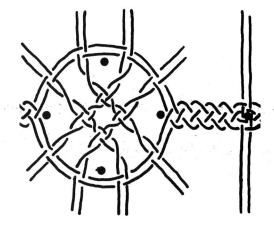

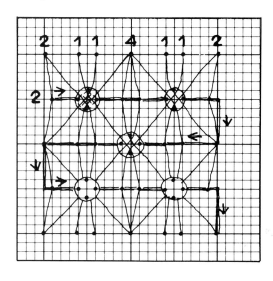

HALOED SPIDER

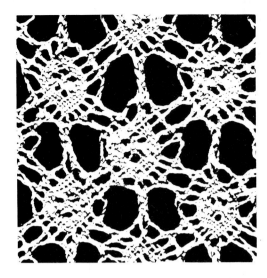

tw. 2, w.s., tw. 2 all legs

braid using each pr as single threads, all
    verticals between buds

pin, w.s. 2 inside prs round pin, tw. 2
    all 4 prs

the inner prs become outside circumference
    prs which w.s., tw. 2 through all legs,
    tw. 2 all legs again

w.s. spider as diagram

note: tw. 3 centre 4 legs before w.s. centre
    and tw. 3 again

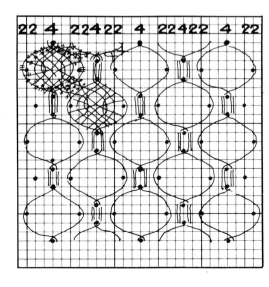

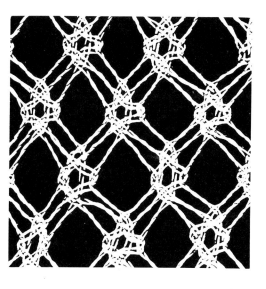

w.s. at top of spider

w.s. next 2 prs through spider passives
  and then through each other

w.s. back out of spider on the opposite
  side

w.s. through next 2 prs, pin, w.s., tw. 1
  at winkie pin

return through spider passives

w.s. through each other in centre

w.s. out through spider passives on
  opposite side

pin and w.s. base of spider

tw. 3 all 6 legs before starting next spider

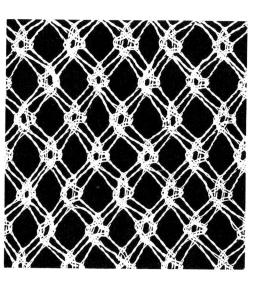

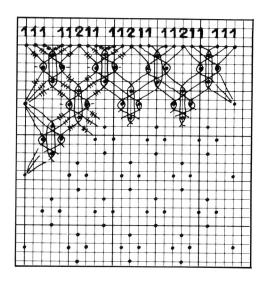

SPIDERS IN HALF STITCH DIAGONALS

h.s. back and forth diagonals picking up
    legs one side and leaving out prs the
    other

junction of diagonals:
    h.s., pin, h.s. 2 centre prs at top of
    pinhole diamond
    h.s., pin, h.s. 2 lt hd prs and 2 rt hd
    prs
    h.s., pin, h.s. 2 centre prs
    tw. 1 all legs before spider and tw. 2
    after

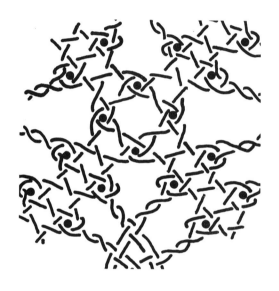

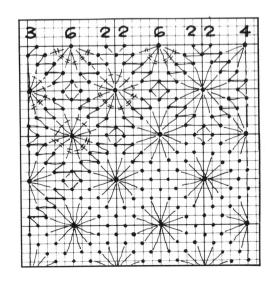

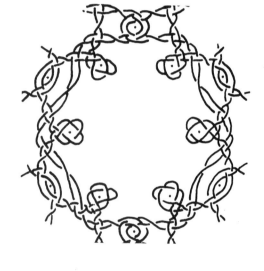

at junction pinholes — w.s., pin, w.s., tw. 1

at picot pinholes — w.s., tw. 1, picot with pr nearest picot, pin, tw. 1, w.s., tw. 1, back through its pr and tw. 1 each pr

with pr nearest pinhole and pr from adjacent pattern w.s., pin, w.s., tw. 1 each pr

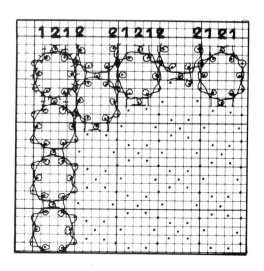

TORCHON STAR

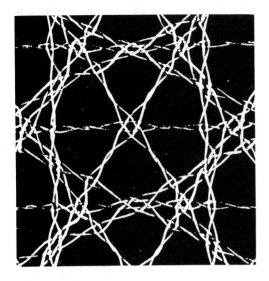

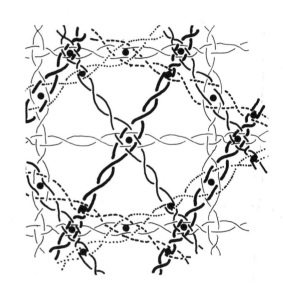

tw. 2 round big star

tw. 1 each other pair

pin in centre of 3 pr cross

w.s. where 2 prs cross

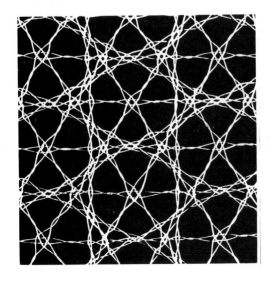

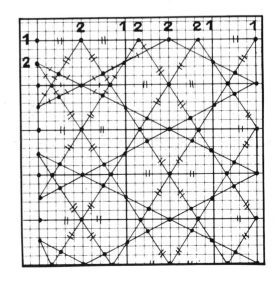

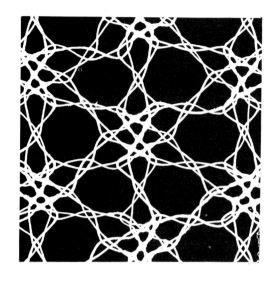

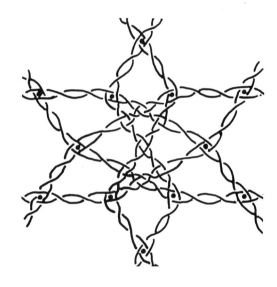

h.s., pin, h.s. at each pinhole
w.s., tw. 1 at all other crossings

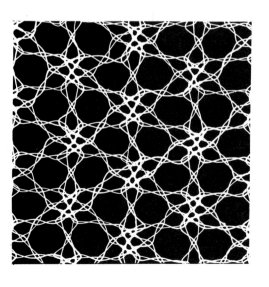

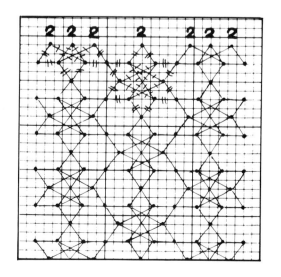

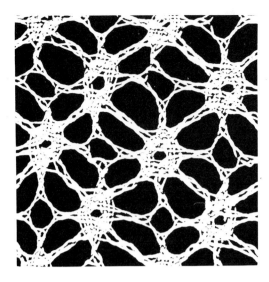

cross inner threads from 1 and 2

w.s. rt hd pr from last stitch to right
   through 2 prs

w.s. 3 through 4 prs to left
w.s. 4 through 5 prs to right
take up pr from 5, w.s. to left through
   2 prs
w.s. 6 to left through 2 prs and leave
w.s. 7 to right through 5 prs
w.s. pr from 1 and 2 to left through 3 prs
w.s. pr from 3 to right through 3 prs
cross last 2 prs

tw. 2 all legs

w.s. with pin in middle at intermediate
   pinholes

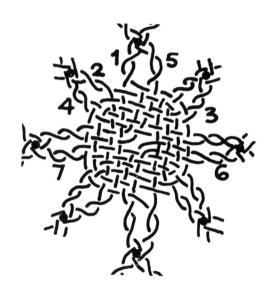

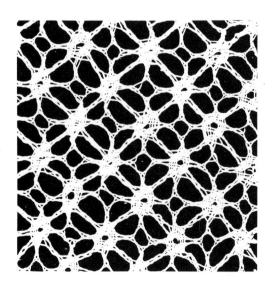

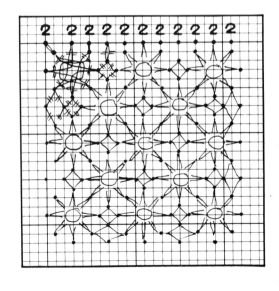

TOILE STAR B

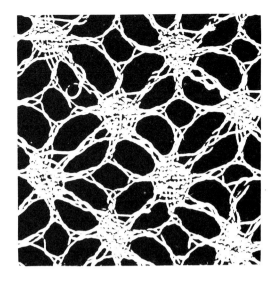

cross inner threads from 1 and 2

w.s. lt hd pr from last st. to lt through
2 prs

w.s. 3 to right through 4 prs

w.s. 4 to left through 5 prs

w.s. 5 to right through 5 prs

w.s. 6 to left through 5 prs

w.s. pr from 1 and 2 to right through
4 prs

w.s. pr from 3 to left through 2 prs

cross last 2 prs

tw. 2 all legs

w.s. with pin in middle at intermediate
pinholes

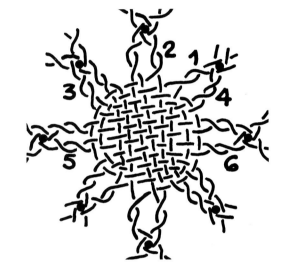

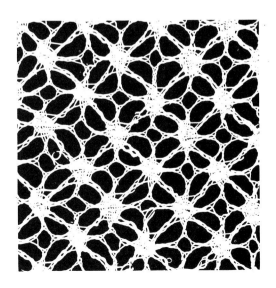

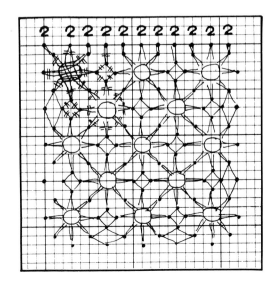

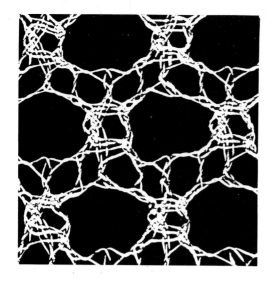

SHELL STAR WITH EXPANDED BRIDES

cross inner threads from 1 and 2

w.s. rt hd pr from last stitch through 2 prs
w.s. 3 to left through 4 prs
w.s. 4 to right through 3 prs, leave
w.s. pr from 1 and 2 with pr from 5

tw. 1 the 2 prs on right of star and braid
these prs x 2 and leave

w.s. pr from 3 to right through 5 prs
w.s. far rt hd pr to left through 2 prs

cross last 2 prs

tw. 2 all legs before and after star

w.s. with pin in middle at intermediate
pinholes

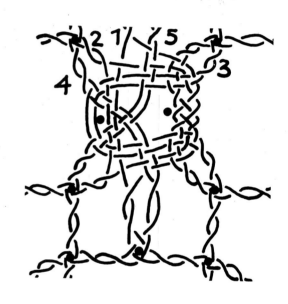

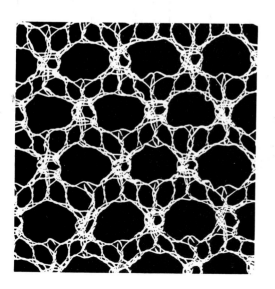

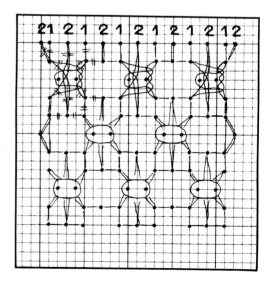

SHELL STAR 1 IN HEXAGONAL FRAME

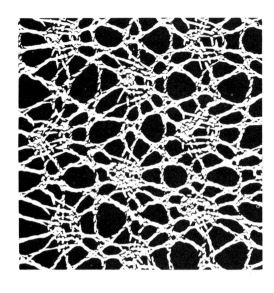

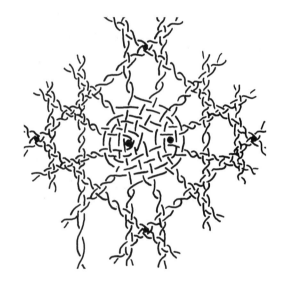

cross inner threads from lt hd pr of lt hd
   diagonal and lt hd pr from vertical
   at start of shell

w.s. throughout as diagram until last
   stitch — h.s. with rt hd diagonal and
   lt hd vertical

tw. 2 all legs from shell

tw. 1 where diagonal and vertical lines
   are close, tw. 2 elsewhere

w.s. with pin in middle where diagonal
   lines cross

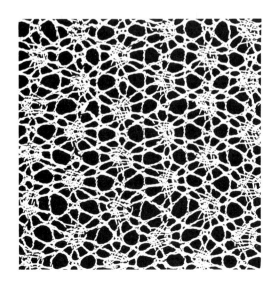

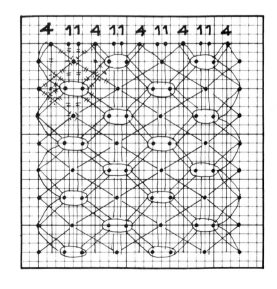

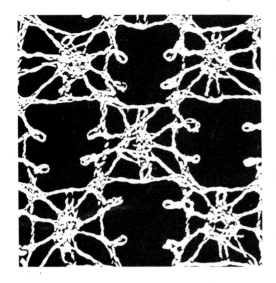

SHELL STAR AND PICOTS

(2) shell star 1:
　　cross inner threads from rt hd pr of lt
　　　hd diagonal and lt hd pr from vertical
　　　at start of shell star
　　w.s. throughout as diagram until last
　　　· stitch, h.s. with rt hd diagonal and
　　　lt hd vertical

(1) frame, top 2 corners (4 prs):
　　w.s. each pr, w.s. centre prs, w.s. outside
　　　prs, w.s. lt 2 prs, w.s. rt 2 prs, tw. 3
　　　all prs

　frame, both sides:
　　with outside pr make large double
　　　picot, tw. 3 both, w.s. with vertical
　　　pr, tw. 3 both

　work shell star (see top rt corner)

　first pr out of star, both sides tw. 3, w.s.
　　with vertical pr, tw. 3 both, make large
　　picot, w.s.
　centre prs from star, tw. 3, pin, w.s., tw. 3
　tw. 3 next prs leaving star before working
　　corner

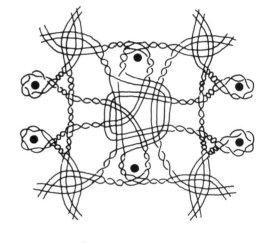

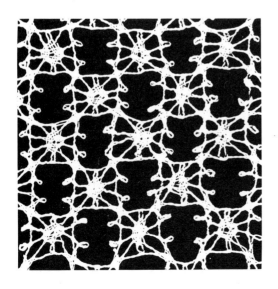

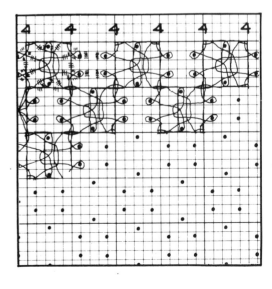

SUNSPOTS

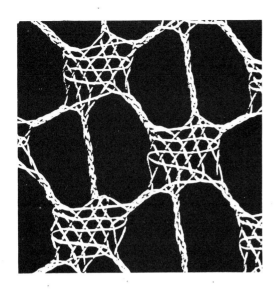

with rt hd pr from vertical braid and lt hd
  pr from next diagonal pr to the right,
  h.s., pin, h.s. at pinhole A

h.s. lt hd pr to pinhole B (picking up 2
  prs from next braid) pin, h.s. to pinholes
  C and D picking up extra prs left out
  before

h.s. to pinhole E, but *not* working last pr

h.s. to pinhole F, again *not* working last pr

close round pin with h.s.

braid all 3 legs until next sunspot

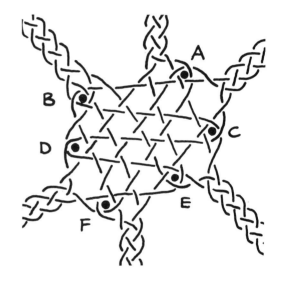

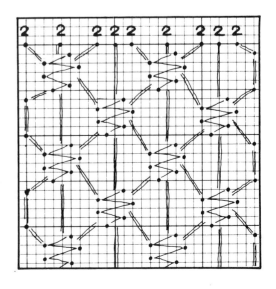

TRENTINO

work horizontally

reverse spiders every other row

w.s., tw. 2 before and after halo

w.s. or h.s. as pattern dictates
1 pr from 5 pr side from top to bottom
    through 3 prs, leave

*take next pr from 5 pr side, w.s. or
    h.s. from top to bottom through 3 prs,
    leave

repeat from * to * 3 more times

braid between spiders

two braids cross with lazy join

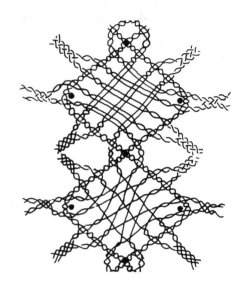

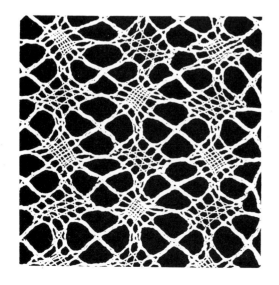

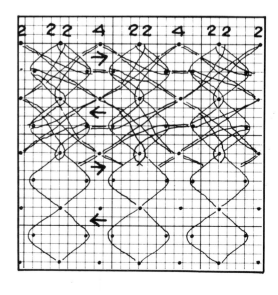

STAR BURST

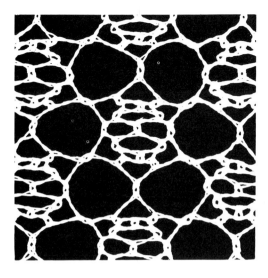

tw. 2 the pairs leading to and from the
  outer points of the star before and
  after they cross

w.s., tw. 1, pin, w.s.

at all other pinholes around and in the
  inner circle w.s., tw. 1, pin, w.s., tw. 1

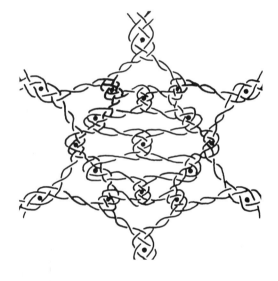

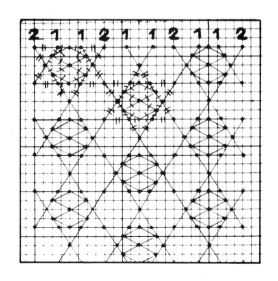

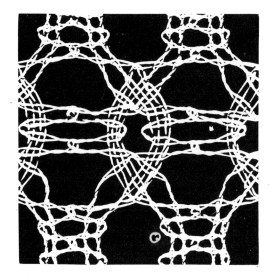

PEA WITH TWISTED BLOCK

w.s. 3 lt hd prs with 3 rt hd prs
w.s. centre lt with 2 lt hd prs
tw. 2, w.s., pin, w.s. with corresponding
    pr from adjacent pea
tw. 2, w.s. rt to centre
tw. 2, pin, w.s. back as above

repeat on right side

w.s. all 3 rt hd prs with lt hd prs
pin before 2 middle prs, w.s. to hold
    shape
tw. 2 centre lt and centre rt

tw. 3 outer prs

w.s., tw. 1 back and forth until next pea

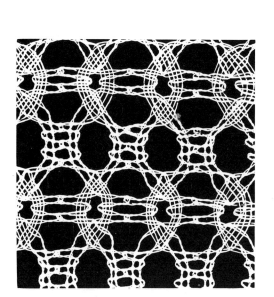

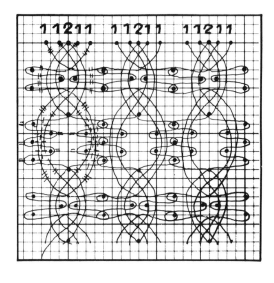

w.s., pin, w.s. prs A and D

w.s. circumference pr A with B and C
   repeat on rt side

w.s. E with B and C; F with B and C

w.s. F with E and A; pin, tw. 2, w.s. F
   back with A and E

w.s. E with A

h.s., pin, h.s. pr E with corresponding
   pr from adjacent pea

w.s. E with A and F; w.s. F with A, pin,
   tw. 2, w.s. pr F with A and E, repeat
   rt side

w.s. centre prs F with C

w.s. C with E and A; w.s. F with B and D

w.s. B with E and A; w.s. E with D

w.s., pin, w.s. circumference prs A and D

tw. 1 all prs out of pea

spiders:
   w.s., pin, w.s. at top of spiders, work
      spider with pin in middle, w.s., pin,
      w.s. at bottom

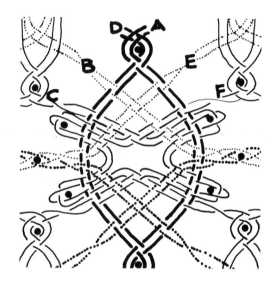

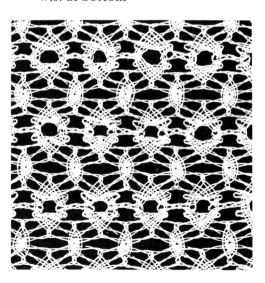

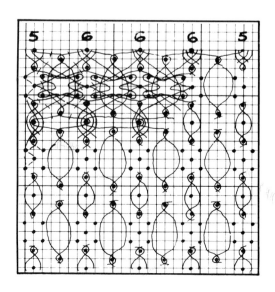

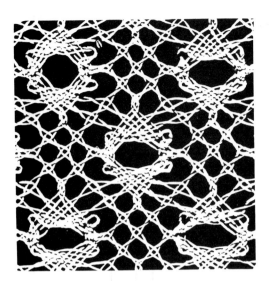

WHOLESTITCH PEA WITH EYELET

w.s., pin, w.s. prs A and D

w.s. circumference pr A with B and C
  repeat on rt side

w.s. E with B and C; F with B and C

w.s. F with E and A, pin, tw. 2, w.s. F
  back with A and E

w.s. E with A

h.s., pin, h.s. pr E with corresponding
  pr from adjacent pea

w.s. E with A and F; w.s. F with A, pin,
  tw. 2., w.s. pr F with A and E, repeat
  on rt side

w.s. centre prs F with C

w.s. C with E and A

w.s. F with B and D

w.s. D with E and A

w.s. E with D

w.s., pin, w.s. circumference prs A and D

tw. 1 all prs out of pea

h.s., pin, h.s. diagonals between

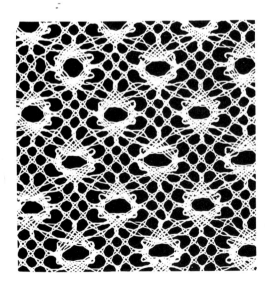

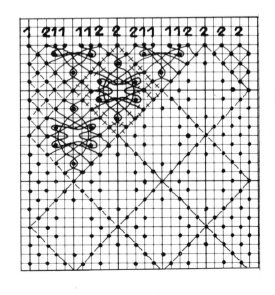